# Royal Pleasures and Pastimes

## CRAFTS FROM THE ROYAL COURTS

# Royal Pleasures and Pastimes

## CRAFTS FROM THE ROYAL COURTS

Julia Jones and Barbara Deer

A DAVID & CHARLES CRAFT BOOK

*For Roger and Pam, Jean and David*

*I know of no person so perfectly disagreeable,*
*and even dangerous, as an author.*
King William IV

*You have got to be careful of Artists.*
*You never know where they have been!*
Queen Victoria

Original photography by Paul Biddle

**British Library Cataloguing in Publication Data**
Jones, Julia *1945–*
    Royal pleasures and pastimes: crafts from the royal
    houses
    1. Great Britain. Queens. Social life, history
    I. Title II. Deer, Barbara
    941.′009′92

ISBN 0–7153–9476–2

Phototypeset by ABM Typographics Ltd, Hull
and printed in Singapore
by C S Graphics Pte Ltd
for David & Charles Publishers plc
Brunel House   Newton Abbot   Devon

Distributed in the United States by
Sterling Publishing Co. Inc,
387 Park Avenue South, New York, NY 10016-8810

# ⊰ CONTENTS ⊱

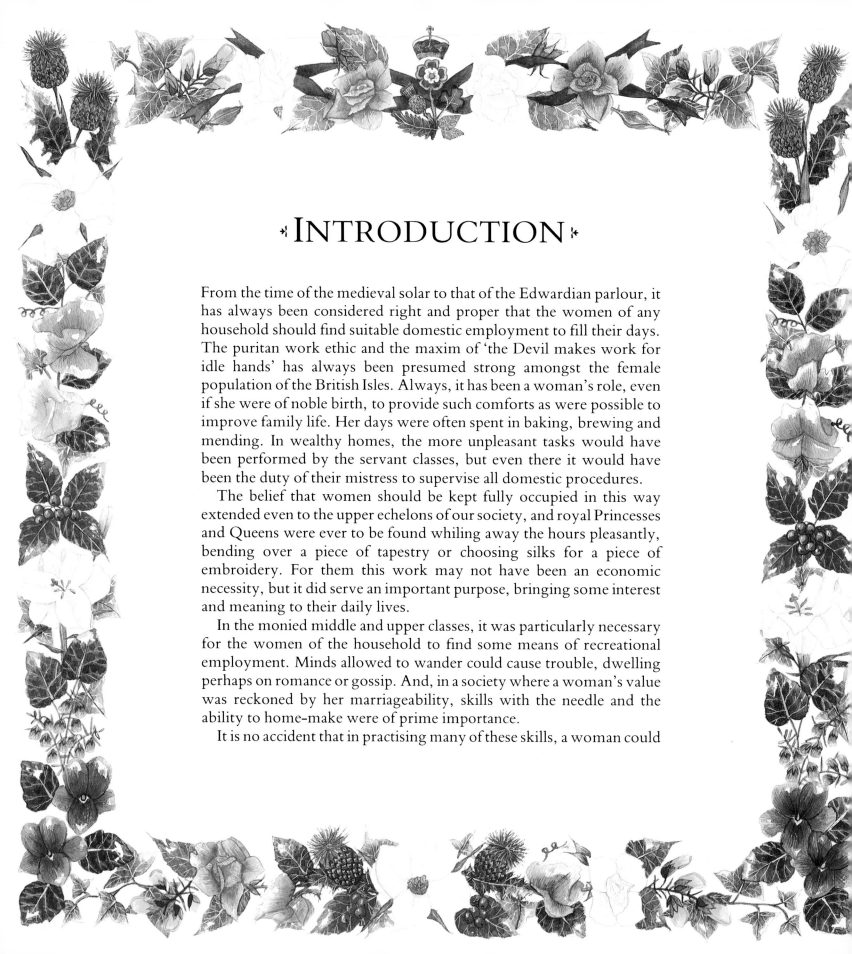

# ⚜ INTRODUCTION ⚜

From the time of the medieval solar to that of the Edwardian parlour, it has always been considered right and proper that the women of any household should find suitable domestic employment to fill their days. The puritan work ethic and the maxim of 'the Devil makes work for idle hands' has always been presumed strong amongst the female population of the British Isles. Always, it has been a woman's role, even if she were of noble birth, to provide such comforts as were possible to improve family life. Her days were often spent in baking, brewing and mending. In wealthy homes, the more unpleasant tasks would have been performed by the servant classes, but even there it would have been the duty of their mistress to supervise all domestic procedures.

The belief that women should be kept fully occupied in this way extended even to the upper echelons of our society, and royal Princesses and Queens were ever to be found whiling away the hours pleasantly, bending over a piece of tapestry or choosing silks for a piece of embroidery. For them this work may not have been an economic necessity, but it did serve an important purpose, bringing some interest and meaning to their daily lives.

In the monied middle and upper classes, it was particularly necessary for the women of the household to find some means of recreational employment. Minds allowed to wander could cause trouble, dwelling perhaps on romance or gossip. And, in a society where a woman's value was reckoned by her marriageability, skills with the needle and the ability to home-make were of prime importance.

It is no accident that in practising many of these skills, a woman could

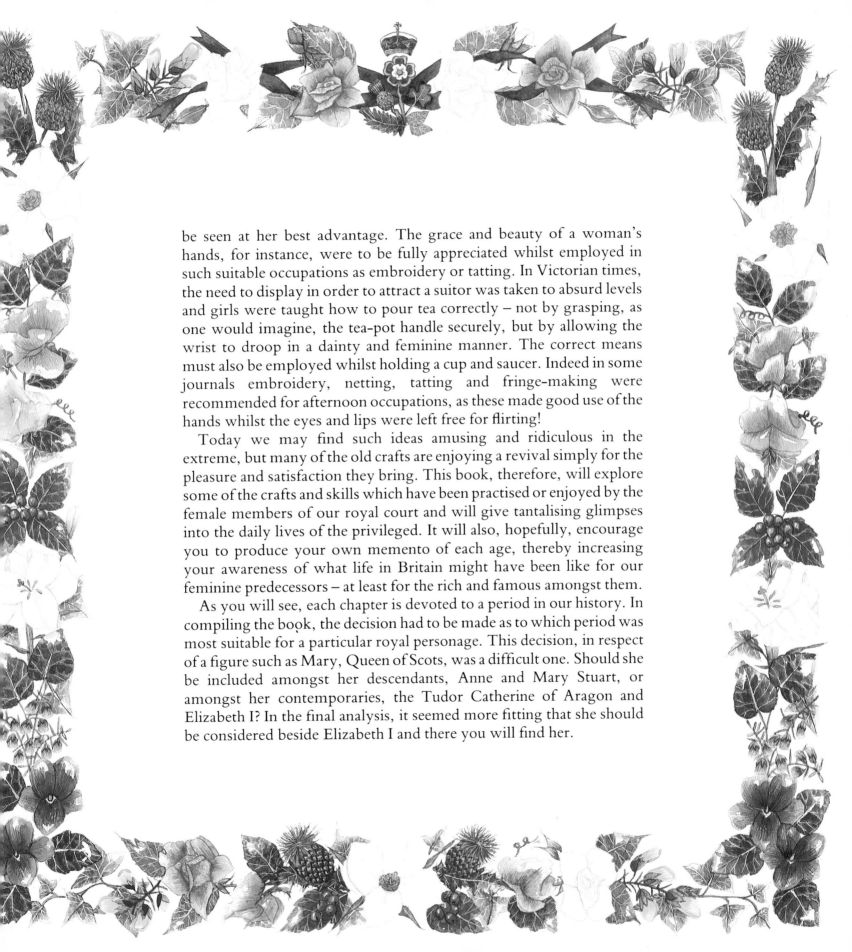

be seen at her best advantage. The grace and beauty of a woman's hands, for instance, were to be fully appreciated whilst employed in such suitable occupations as embroidery or tatting. In Victorian times, the need to display in order to attract a suitor was taken to absurd levels and girls were taught how to pour tea correctly – not by grasping, as one would imagine, the tea-pot handle securely, but by allowing the wrist to droop in a dainty and feminine manner. The correct means must also be employed whilst holding a cup and saucer. Indeed in some journals embroidery, netting, tatting and fringe-making were recommended for afternoon occupations, as these made good use of the hands whilst the eyes and lips were left free for flirting!

Today we may find such ideas amusing and ridiculous in the extreme, but many of the old crafts are enjoying a revival simply for the pleasure and satisfaction they bring. This book, therefore, will explore some of the crafts and skills which have been practised or enjoyed by the female members of our royal court and will give tantalising glimpses into the daily lives of the privileged. It will also, hopefully, encourage you to produce your own memento of each age, thereby increasing your awareness of what life in Britain might have been like for our feminine predecessors – at least for the rich and famous amongst them.

As you will see, each chapter is devoted to a period in our history. In compiling the book, the decision had to be made as to which period was most suitable for a particular royal personage. This decision, in respect of a figure such as Mary, Queen of Scots, was a difficult one. Should she be included amongst her descendants, Anne and Mary Stuart, or amongst her contemporaries, the Tudor Catherine of Aragon and Elizabeth I? In the final analysis, it seemed more fitting that she should be considered beside Elizabeth I and there you will find her.

# ⚜CHAPTER I⚜

# The Normans

I order all Rattons that be in this House,
All mannere of Rattons, and eke of Mouse,
By the grace of Mary cleane –
Go hence Rattons! and be no more seene –
And by Him, whom Mary bare aboute,
Let no Ratton stay! within or withoute,
And by the Holy Ghost of grace,
That all Rattons! leave this place!
By the Father, and the Sone –
I bid all Rattons, to be Gone . . .

Medieval Household Charm

# MATILDA OF FLANDERS

*Wife of William the Conqueror*

Not a great deal is known of Queen Matilda. She was the daughter of Count Baldwin of Flanders and Adelais, daughter of the King of France. It is said that she at first rejected William's offer of marriage on the grounds that he was a bastard and the son of a tanner's daughter. Hearing of her rejection, William apparently responded by riding to Flanders, where he is said to have beaten Matilda soundly, pulling her from her horse by her long, golden hair which hung in braids over each shoulder.

This incident amazingly, far from increasing Matilda's dislike of the match, caused her to regret her impulsive insults and she agreed to become Duchess of Normandy. She was married amidst much rejoicing at Rouen in 1053, despite the threat of excommunication from the Pope, who feebly declared that the couple were distant cousins. Chroniclers of the time wrote that Matilda was both beautiful and gifted with great abilities, many of which, being a woman, she was unable to use. Matilda, however, was a Princess directly descended from Alfred the Great, and as such, her marriage to William reinforced his claim to the English throne.

During her life Matilda became the patroness of many churches and as gifts she often gave examples of her own embroidery. The Holy Trinity church at Caen in Normandy received her gold embroidered mantle, which was later turned into a cape.

At his birth, William's mother had prophesied that her son would be the greatest-ever Duke of Normandy and that he would rule a kingdom over the seas. Whilst pregnant, she had dreamed that a giant tree grew from her stomach and that its branches spread wide, shading many countries. In order to fulfil this prophesy, William landed in England in 1066, fighting and defeating King Harold at Senlac Hill (Battle of Hastings). This victory began the Norman Conquest and radically changed the lives of our Saxon ancestors. Very shortly after William's success, the Norman court took up residence in England and with his knights came Norman ladies with their embroideries, Norman cooks

9

with their new dishes and Norman architects with their new plans. Life in England was never to be the same again. The new King even tried to force his reluctant subjects to speak Norman French rather than Anglo-Saxon.

## ⚜ THE BAYEUX TAPESTRY ⚜

Tradition has it that 'it was Matilda, Queen of England, Duchess of Normandy, who wove it (the Tapestry) herself with her ladies-in-waiting'. As a skilled needlewoman, it was believed that the Queen took pleasure in 'depicting through her own handiwork, the most dazzling achievement of the life of Duke William'. This would have made Matilda into a sort of Norman 'Penelope', and from this charming legend comes the work's nineteenth-century name of 'Queen Matilda's Tapestry'. If the Bayeux Tapestry was truly the work of the ladies of the Norman court, it shows a remarkable understanding of weaponry and ships, but perhaps it was drawn for them by professional designers? The mystery has never been adequately solved.

The Bayeux Tapestry is, nevertheless, a remarkable piece of embroidery. It is 230ft (70m) long and 20in (50cm) wide and records events from the accession of Edward the Confessor to the downfall of Harold. It portrays no less than 1,255 figures, some of which are quite crudely represented. It can in no way be technically considered the finest needlework of its time, but as a social record it is invaluable showing, as it does, all aspects of life in the eleventh century.

## ⚜ A WOMAN'S LOT ⚜

Women in Norman times did not have many rights. Although they could inherit land, even the most noble of ladies could not testify in court, or even make a will without her husband's permission. The King had power over all women, and widows could be forced to re-marry or forfeit their inheritance at his pleasure.

An unmarried daughter was considered something of a liability in a Norman household, and every effort was made to arrange a suitable (or sometimes totally unsuitable) marriage for her. William and Matilda's

daughter, Adelisa, was betrothed at just ten years of age to Harold, Earl of Wessex, as part of his oath of loyalty. As a prisoner in Normandy, Harold was forced to pledge his support in making William King of England on the death of Edward the Confessor. However, as this oath was extracted under duress and was a condition of his release, Harold felt entitled to break it on his return to England, claiming the throne for himself and marrying elsewhere. The young Adelisa was thought never to have recovered from her disappointment, for she died on board the ship carrying her to a new alliance with the King of Galicia. She was just eleven years old at the time.

In noble households, if a younger daughter should marry before her older sister, it was customary for this older girl to wear green stockings at the ceremony as a symbol of grief and shame. If no suitable suitor could be found for her, the only honourable course for a spinster was the convent life, as a bride of Christ.

# ⚜ EMBROIDERY ⚜

The main craft for which the Norman period is famous is the embroidered and applied work which was practised in many religious houses. It was mainly undertaken by monks and nuns. Indeed, it appears that the nuns at this time so enjoyed their needlework, that they were in danger of forgetting their immortal souls and could often be found excusing themselves from divine service in order to finish a particularly attractive and interesting piece of work. Nuns usually came from the richer families for a convent life was often a convenient method of disposing of the illegitimate or unmarried daughters of noble houses. The heavy work in nunneries, therefore, was always carried out by lay servants, the nuns' time being given over to more genteel and leisurely pursuits. Yet embroidery must have been a fairly tedious business in Norman times; crude iron needles meant that the working threads were often worn through and so needed constant attention. The Church, however, secured a considerable income from commissions for the needlework thus produced, and in the poorer establishments nuns complained that too many orders were being taken, causing them to suffer from overwork.

From the sixth century onwards the Church became established in Britain and thus developed the famous English metal-thread embroideries of the Middle Ages. Much use was made of gold and silver thread and, in many cases, even precious jewels were sewn on to the fabric. By the twelfth century this English work was becoming recognised as the best of its kind in Europe.

The use of metal threads in this way is as old as the craft of the goldsmith and the weaver. Pure gold was beaten into thin sheets and then cut into extremely thin strips. It was then pliable enough to work into warps, stitch through open-weave fabrics or to wind around a silken core to use as a couching thread.

Embroidery in the home was still considered basically a useful craft. Early examples exist which show it in use joining narrow strips of fabric together, much as we would machine stitch today. It was also used for strengthening and reinforcing garments against wear. Quilted padding was needed to protect a knight's body from chafing under heavy armour, and embroidery was put to more decorative use to personalise banners and horse trappings with coats of arms. The Church also used embroidery as an early form of teaching aid, explaining Bible stories to the illiterate.

Embroidered garments were the privilege of the wealthy. So important was the right to wear decorated fabrics considered, that a law was passed forbidding the wearing of these clothes by any person with an income of less than £200 a year (a considerable amount in the Middle Ages). In the main, clothing for most people was dull and purely functional. Display in dress was not thought generally desirable until much later.

## Netted Work

A craft which would have been enjoyed by the ladies of the court was a form of netted work. In this technique, a darned pattern was worked over a piece of net. This fabric was then used to make veils, nets for the hair and caps. Fine examples worked in silk have been recorded from as early as 1092.

A crespin or caul to contain the hair was indispensible to a married

lady of fashion and, as time progressed, the ornamentation on these articles became much more elaborate.

The hair of a fashionable unmarried lady of court would, however, be parted in the middle of the head and plaited into two long tresses, much as the young Matilda would have done. These tresses were often 'gallooned', which meant that the hair was divided into several tufts which were then embroidered with gold or silver thread.

## Legal Needles

Meanwhile, embroidery at the Welsh court was the right of only a few. There were only three so-called 'legal' needles in the land. One was used by the chief huntsman to sew up wounded dogs, one belonged in the equipment of the palace doctor and the other was kept for the Queen's needlework. Each of these needles, which would have been made of iron, was valued at 4d.

Steel sewing needles would not be available in Britain until the sixteenth century, when they appeared at Queen Mary's court for the first time, brought, apparently, by a Spanish Moor all the way from India.

*My fair long straight needle, that was mine only treasure*
*The first day of my sorrow is, and last of my pleasure.*
*The Loss of Gammer Gurton's Needle* (1575)

# ⊹ WASHDAY ⊹

The washing of clothes must have presented quite a problem to the Norman housewife. Before the widespread use of soap, bundles of the aptly named herb, soapwort, were boiled in water until 'sudsy' and this was then used for laundering the family linen. Balls of fern were burned until they became what was known as 'blewish', and this ash was then dissolved in water to improve the colour of white linen (a forerunner of the Victorian blue-bag).

In noble houses, rosewater was often included in the washing of fine linen to add a gentle perfume. To produce true rosewater is a long and complicated business, involving the use of a still. However, a passable substitute can be easily made at home.

## To Make Rosewater

*2 handfuls of scented rose petals*
*225g (8oz) sugar*
*1 litre (2pts) boiling water*

Put the rose petals into an earthenware pot. Dissolve the sugar in the boiling water. Leave to cool until tepid. Pour over the rose petals. Leave to infuse for 1 hour. Stir gently but thoroughly. Leave for another hour. Strain and bottle. Kept in the fridge, this rosewater will last for about a week. Use in finger bowls or in the rinsing water of fine linens.

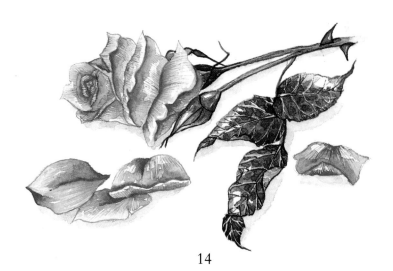

14

# ⚜ THE STILLROOM ⚜

Medicine and the care of the sick was still a strange mixture of ridiculous remedies and real knowledge. In the main, the religious houses provided the only practical help during an illness, with their regime of relatively wholesome food, kindly ministrations and comparative cleanliness. This, combined with potions made from the herbs grown in their gardens, must have helped many who had lost hope of ever regaining their health. In the home, the lady of the house would have grown what herbs she could, pounding and boiling them to provide remedies to cure both family and livestock.

Surgery was regarded, needless to say, as the last resort and was completely separate from medicine. As such it was performed by the uneducated, mainly as a sideline for tradesmen such as barbers and bath-keepers. A surgeon who was called upon to operate on his lord or lady risked death if the operation proved unsuccessful, so it can be imagined that there was no great rush to take on this honour. Operating techniques were of necessity primitive in the extreme, especially if performed by the itinerate practitioners who went from village to village offering their services. There were, of course, no anaesthetics, but sleeping draughts such as hemlock, opium or mandragora (mandrake) would hopefully have been administered to deaden the pain.

The mandrake was believed to be a herb with special magical powers. Its roots were often forked and it was said that as it was pulled from the ground it shrieked in pain. The resemblance of the twisted roots to the human form meant that it was often used in charms and witchcraft, and it was once widely rumoured to be a powerful aphrodisiac.

# ⚜ ROYAL GARDENS ⚜

Royal gardens had their 'herbers' or pleasure grounds, planted with sweet-smelling flowers and herbs. Many of the flowers still grown today were to be seen there. It may be that Queen Eleanor, who was with Edward I on his Crusade, brought the hollyhock to England from the Holy Land, but another inhabitant of our cottage gardens, the

wallflower, is said to have been introduced by the Normans. Indeed it can still often be seen growing around their castle ruins today. Medieval gardens also included roses and the sweet-smelling pinks which were believed to be the favourite flowers of William the Conqueror.

The design of the herbers was based on geometric shapes, usually large squares or rectangles. They were always walled in or surrounded by thick hedges. Within these walls the square or rectangle, known as the 'flowery mede', was filled with grass and a host of different flowers. The words 'meadow' and 'mede' come from the same source, the Anglo-Saxon word *mede* meaning to be mown by the mouth of a sheep. The ornamental lawn as we know it was not introduced until the first mechanical mowers were invented in Victorian times.

It was, however, becoming increasingly fashionable to plant orchards, although the Normans considered fruit unwholesome, unless eaten on an empty stomach. Pears were believed to be particularly harmful, unless taken with a large goblet of wine.

In the Middle Ages it was believed possible to tell the hour of day by the use of flowers, which were supposed to open and close at specific times. These would be planted in flower dials. The first hour belonged to the budding rose, the fourth to hyacinths and the twelfth to pansies. The unreliability of this method of time keeping must have soon become apparent, but floral clocks can still be seen planted in parks and gardens today.

*Breakfast at five*
*Dinner at ten*
*Supper at five*
*Bed by seven*
Advice for a Healthy and Prosperous Life

17

*The Situation thereof. Amongst the noble Cities of the World, honoured by Fame, the City of London is the one principal Seat of the Kingdom of England, whose Renown is spread abroad very far; but she transporteth her Wares and Commodities much farther, and advanceth her Head so much the higher. Happy she is in the Wholesomeness of the Air, in the Christian Religion, her munition also and Strength, the nature of her situation, the Honour of her Citizens, the Chastity of her Matrons; very plentiful also in her Sports and Pastimes and replenished with honourable Personages. All of which I think meet severally to consider.*

*The Temperateness of the Air. In this Place, the Calmness of the Air doth mollify Men's Minds, not corrupting them with Lusts, but preserving them from savage and rude behaviour, and seasoning their Inolinations with a more kind and free Temper.*

William Fitzstephen (died c1190)
*A Description of the Most Honourable City of London*

# ⊹ THE GREAT HALL ⊹

Life after the Norman invasion must have been very unsettled for the Anglo-Saxon community. Communications were difficult and most people would have had a hard struggle to make life comfortable for themselves and their children. During the eleventh century each manor house would have needed to be self-sufficient, providing all the basic necessities of life for its owners and their servants. Bread had to be baked in the bakehouse from corn grown in the fields. Ale was brewed in the brewhouse, butter and cheese made in the dairy, while in the larder candles were made, bacon cured and meat salted down. Even clothes and household linen were fashioned from cloth woven at home. The ladies of most households had little time to spend in recreation, each waking moment being surely devoted to providing life's essentials for their families.

The great hall of Norman times was the main living-room of the

castle, where everyone met together. Around the hall, and built as a gallery, were various small rooms. These were used by the family as bedchambers. Often they did not have windows but, to provide a little privacy, leather curtains were hung over the entrance doors. Servants slept on rushes strewn on the floor below. The constant noise and lack of solitude must have been quite a problem.

The Normans loved music. At mealtimes, minstrels were employed to walk before the kitchen servants and these musicians would continue to play thoughout the meal. Harpists and poets would be called upon to entertain and bands of acrobats and tumblers would enter, as the meal progressed, to perform their displays.

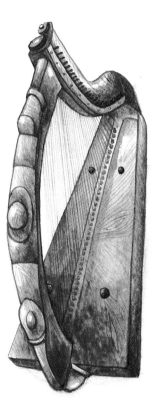

*The knife is in the food, drink is in the horn*
*and there is rejoicing in the hall and no-one*
*may enter the Court of Arthur unless he is a*
*King of a free country or a craftsman plying a craft.*

From the *Mabinogion,* Welsh Folk Stories

# ⚜ THE NORMAN DINING TABLE ⚜

Norman mealtimes were extremely messy occasions by today's standards. Eating implements and table manners were very basic and so it became customary for the sophisticated to dip their hands into scented water after a meal, to remove grease and odours from the fingers. This practice had been common amongst the nobility even in the Dark Ages, when personal hygiene was not high on the list of priorities!

To sit down to dinner at a Norman table, each diner would be required to bring their own set of eating implements, usually a knife, various spoons and a spike. This set of cutlery was known as a 'nef', and as soon as a child was old enough to dine in the Hall, he or she would be presented with their very own 'nef' and also a drinking goblet. It is interesting to note that a set of cutlery and a christening mug are still considered suitable as christening presents today.

The narrow, Norman dining tables would be covered with square cloths, laid diagonally. This method of laying the table meant that a

triangle of cloth overhung on each side. This overlapping triangle was conveniently placed for the wiping of greasy hands and, as the years passed, diners tucked these ends under their chins. Napkins were placed over the left shoulder of the diner, or tied, like a bib, around the neck. The more refined Normans shaped these napkins into elaborate and extravagant designs, often perfuming them with rosewater and changing them for each course. Before each meal a groom would lay the table, taking with him extra napkins shaped in a 'stately' way. The bishop would get a 'mitre', the traveller 'a shoe' and the ladies a 'fleur-de-lys', a 'rose' or a 'jousting token'. The elaborate folding of napkins today is still that of the medieval banqueting table.

## *To Fold a Table Napkin*

To work successfully, the napkin should be square, preferably but not necessarily about 75 x 75cm (30 x 30in). It should be lightly starched and ironed smooth. As these designs are quite complicated, it may be as well to practise on a piece of paper until the method is fully understood.

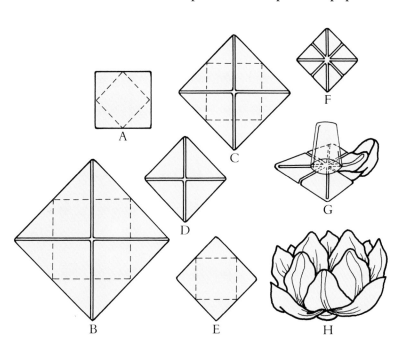

**The Rose** (left) Place the napkin on a flat surface and fold in each corner as shown in A. Moving the napkin a quarter turn, again fold in the four corners (B). Turn again and fold in the corners yet again (C). continue in this manner until F has been completed. Turn face downwards and hold a tumbler firmly in the middle of the napkin (G). Carefully pull up points around the tumbler to create the shape shown in H. A bread roll can be placed in the centre of the rose.

**The Fleur-de-lys** (right) Fold the napkin in half crossways, from corner to corner, as shown in A, then fold down one-third from this folded edge (B). The two points are then folded back on themselves (C). To finish, push the bottom edge into a wine glass or napkin ring and arrange points to form the fleur-de-lys (D).

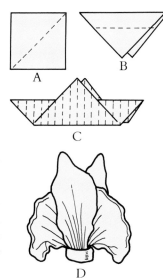

# ✢ THE DAIRY ✢

*Little Miss Muffett,*
*Sat on a tuffet*
*Eating her curds and whey.*
*There came a big spider*
*Who sat down beside her*
*And frightened Miss Muffet away.*
Children's Nursery Rhyme

## Curds and Whey
To make 12oz

*600ml (1pt) pasteurised milk*
*50g (2oz) milk powder*
*1 x 5ml tsp (1 tsp) rennet essence*

Heat the milk in a double saucepan until it reaches 38°C (100°F). Stir in the milk powder, followed by the rennet essence. Cover and leave for 1 hour to set to form curd.

Line a sieve with double-thickness butter muslin and stand over a bowl. Ladle thin slices of curd into the sieve. The watery liquid which appears is the whey. Gather the corners of the muslin together and tie to make a bag. Hang on a hook with a bowl beneath and leave to drain for 4-5 hours. Turn out and pour fresh cream over. Sprinkle with caster sugar and serve.

Milk and milk products were known as 'white meat' and were considered to be the food of the poor or the sick. The word we know as 'junket' comes from the Norman French *jonchée*, a little rush basket used to strain the curds from the whey. A Norman blancmange would have been a curious dish in which white meat was pounded to a pulp and mixed with almonds, milk, boiled rice and sugar. Not perhaps suited to modern tastes.

21

# ⚜THE KITCHEN⚜

In the Bayeux Tapestry cooks are shown busily at work in the kitchen, boiling a pot over one fire and spit-roasting over another. The prepared meat was then carried to the table by Saxon serfs, to be eaten by their Norman lords.

It is interesting to note that the names still used for our domestic animals are old Saxon words, but their flesh has for centuries been known by its Norman-derived name. The defeated Saxons, naturally, had the job of tending the domestic animals, but it was the Normans who enjoyed their meat at table. The only exception to this appears to have been 'bacon', which may have appeared as a Saxon supper dish from time to time.

| SAXON | NORMAN |
|---|---|
| ox, cow | beef |
| calf | veal |
| sheep | mutton |
| swine | pork |
| fowl | pullet |
| deer | venison |

## Norman Recipes

*The love of a woman and a bottle of wine*
*Are sweet for a season and last for a time!*

Norman proverb

A popular accompaniment to wine or ale were wafers, often sold by street traders called 'waferers'. The medieval wafer was very similar to modern waffles.

### Wafers

*100g (4oz) plain flour*
*pinch of salt*
*7g (¼oz) fresh yeast*
*150ml (¼pt) warm milk*
*1 x 5ml tsp (1tsp) sugar*
*1 egg*
*50g (2oz) melted butter*
*1 x 5ml tsp (1tsp) rosewater*

Sift the flour and salt into a bowl. Dissolve the yeast with the warm milk and sugar. Add all ingredients to the flour and mix well. Leave for 1 hour. Meanwhile, heat a pan of cooking oil and heat and grease the

waffle iron. When hot, dip the iron into the batter and transfer quickly to the pan. As the waffle cooks it will slip off the iron. Leave to fry until golden brown. Remove with a slotted spoon. Drain and serve with jam and cream or sprinkled with caster sugar.

This recipe is written using an old-fashioned waffle iron. It is possible, however, to use the batter to make waffles in an electric waffle iron. Do be careful not to pour in too much mixture; it is important to realise that the mixture will rise considerably as it cooks.

## *Medieval Chewing Wax*

This is an authentic recipe and, as such, is interesting to try. It will not, however, be acceptable to most modern tastes!

*1 honeycomb OR 1 cup of beeswax and 1 x 15ml tbsp (1tbsp) honey*
*½ x 5ml tsp (½tsp) ginger OR cinnamon*
*1 drop oil of terebinth (optional)★*

Melt the honeycomb, or the wax and the honey. Mix in the spice and oil. Heat to just below boiling point. Beat well until cool and pour into moulds to set.

★Oil of terebinth is the old name for turpentine and will give the chewing wax an authentic flavour of pine-tree resin, but is not recommended!

# ⚜ CANDLE-MAKING ⚜

In poor homes, lighting would have been erratic to say the least. Tapers and rushes dipped in tallow fat or lard would have provided a little light for emergencies. Candles made from grease of this sort produced a good deal of evil-smelling smoke and so were not a practical method of constant illumination. In the 1300s, a slight improvement was made to these tapers by dipping splinters of wood into fat, thus providing a slightly more reliable candle.

The rich, however, were able to indulge in the luxury of lighting their supper tables with torches and candles made from beeswax. These beeswax candles were far superior to the tallow varieties. They were

easily made and gave off a pleasant, clean smoke with a sweet perfume. Their soft, flickering glow must have been very welcome in wintertime, especially during the long dark after-dinner hours.

## An Hour Candle

*700g (24oz) paraffin wax*
*60g (2¹/₂oz) stearin*
*6cm (2¹/₂in) plastic piping*
*plasticine*
*plastic lid from yoghurt pot*
*or something similar*
*38cm (16in) medium weight smooth string*
*boracic powder*
*black enamel paint*
*2cm (³⁄₄in) drafting tape*

Prepare the plastic piping by brushing the inside with a little olive oil.

Mix 1 teaspoon of boracic powder with a little water and soak the string, which should then be hung up and left to dry. Tie a tight knot in one end of the string.

Using a skewer, make a hole in the centre of the yoghurt pot lid and thread the string through until anchored by the knot. Seal the hole with a little plasticine. Put the tube over the lid and seal it firmly around with plasticine to make sure none of the hot wax can escape. Bring the string up the tube to form the wick and tie firmly to a pencil. Secure this pencil across the rim of the tube with a little extra plasticine, making sure that the wick will be in the centre of the finished candle. Place the prepared mould in a jug or vase to keep it upright and pack round with cotton wool or tissue paper.

Put the paraffin wax into a double boiler and heat gently. The wax is ready when it reaches 75°C (170°F). Take care not to let it boil. In a separate saucepan melt the stearin and, when it is liquid, add it to the paraffin wax. Now carefully pour the wax into the mould and leave for twenty-four hours to cool.

To remove the candle from the mould, cut the knot from the string and remove the yoghurt top and plasticine, then pull on the pencil until the candle is released. If this does not work, dip the mould briefly into hot water and try again. Trim the wick and leave the candle to cool again for 30 minutes.

Stick a band of 2cm (³⁄₄in) wide drafting tape around the lower edge of the candle as a guideline and paint a black band around the candle using the enamel paint. Remove the tape and, using the previous mark as a guide, continue marking rings at 2cm (³⁄₄in) intervals up the entire length of the candle. Then paint on the Roman numberals as shown in the photograph opposite.

## A Simple Beeswax Candle

*sheet of beeswax*
*string OR wick*

Beeswax can be bought in sheets, so that the more complicated procedures for candle-making can be eliminated. Take a sheet of wax and with a sharp knife cut it to the required height of the finished candle. Put the sheet on a flat surface and place the wick at one end. The wick should be slightly longer than the sheet. Very carefully roll the wick up in the sheet until the required thickness is obtained. Cut off the surplus with the knife. To finish off, press the end of the sheet into the body of the candle, using the warmth from your hands to smooth the wax until the candle is perfectly cylindrical. Trim the wick and level the bottom of the candle with the knife.

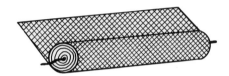

# ⁂ THE SMALLEST ROOM ⁂

The sanitary arrangements in a Norman castle were primitive in the extreme. The lavatories or garderobes, often conveniently placed in an angle opposite the staircase, consisted merely of a shaft built into the thickness of the outer walls. They must have been exceedingly unpleasant, despite the fact that experience eventually caused them to be ventilated by small windows. With domestic offices so basic, it is not surprising that perfume seemed to be the main preoccupation of most noble ladies!

# MATILDA
### *Daughter of Henry I*
### (1102-1167)

Henry I is said to have fathered at least twenty-one children, but unfortunately for England only two were born in wedlock. His only legitimate son, William, perished at sea in the sinking of the 'White Ship' as it returned from Normandy, leaving his daughter Matilda – she was christened Maud but became generally known as Matilda – to

represent the direct line of the Dukes of Normandy.

Matilda had left England when she was only eight years old to become the wife of Henry V, the Holy Roman Emperor. She was widowed in 1125, and returned to England to marry Geoffrey Plantagenet, Count of Anjou. Amongst her wedding gifts, it is recorded that she received a silver peacock set with precious stones. This ornamental bird was designed to hold rosewater at banquets.

Despite the seeming incompatibility of the couple, Matilda was twenty-five and Geoffrey only fourteen at the time of their marriage, they managed to produce three children. The eldest, Henry Plantagenet, was born on the 5 March 1133. The family name of Plantagenet appears to have been taken by Henry's father, who ordered broom (planta genista) to be planted in order to improve the hunting cover on his lands. Broom became a symbol of this Royal dynasty.

Matilda had never been popular in England, even as a child. She was to become a disagreeable woman, avaricious, haughty and tactless. Although heiress to the throne of England, the barons did not take kindly to the idea of being ruled by a woman, especially Matilda. However, before his death her father called together these men, forcing them to take an oath upholding her as their future Queen.

Then one day, whilst out hunting in the forests around Lyons, Henry I was seized by an acute attack of indigestion, brought on, some say, by eating too many lampreys. Fever rapidly set in and the King died on 1 December 1135. At the news of Henry's death, the powerful barons turned their eyes towards Stephen, Count of Blois, Henry's nephew. At their request Stephen slipped across the channel to be crowned King.

Having lost her claim to the English throne, Matilda decided to turn her attention towards Normandy in an attempt to establish her rights there. The Normans, however, were no keener than the English to have this woman as their sovereign and so she returned once again to England, in September 1139, to challenge Stephen. This caused civil war, which was to last until February 1148 when she at last gave up the fight and returned to Normandy.

The death of Stephen when it came in 1154 was too late for Matilda but it did leave the way open for her son, as Henry II, to become the first of the Plantagenet kings.

# * CHAPTER II *

# The Plantagenets

One day Queen Eleanor saw the King walking in the pleasance of Woodstock, with the end of a ball of floss silk attached to his spur, and that coming near him unperceived, she took up the ball, and the King walking onward, the silk unwound, and thus the Queen traced him to a thicket in the labyrinth or maze of the park, where he disappeared. She kept the matter secret, after revolving in her own mind in what company he could meet with balls of silk. Soon after the King left Woodstock for a distant journey, then Queen Eleanor, bearing this discovery in mind, searched the thicket in the park, and found a low door cunningly concealed; this door she had forced, and found it was the entrance to a winding, subterranean path, which led out at a distance to a sylvan lodge in the most lovely part of the adjoining forest.

John Brompton of Gervanix
'On the Discovery by Queen Eleanor of Aquitaine of Rosamund Clifford, mistress of her husband Henry II',
*Chronicle 588–1199* (c1458)

*We came from the Devil, and to the Devil we will return!*

King Richard I on his family

# ELEANOR OF AQUITAINE
*Wife of Henry II*
(1122–1202)

Eleanor was married to Louis VII of France at the tender age of fifteen. At that time, it was expected that a lady should be able to hawk, play chess and relate stories. She should also have the intelligence to respond to banter with witty repartee, have a sweet singing voice and be able to play at least one musical instrument. It was also assumed that she should be able to read and write. Eleanor was accomplished in all such feminine pursuits.

Her unhappy marriage to Louis was to last for fifteen years, during which time Eleanor bore the King two daughters. This marriage was annulled, however, in 1152 when Eleanor became enamoured of the young Henry of Normandy, who must have seemed a god compared with the saintly and studious Louis. Two months after her divorce Eleanor and Henry were married.

On the death of King Stephen, who left no heir, Henry and Eleanor became King and Queen of England. Theirs was a tempestuous relationship, aggravated surely by Henry's numerous affairs. It is said that his liaison with Rosamund Clifford, the 'Fair Rosamund', caused untold damage to their marriage and when Rosamund died in mysterious circumstances, Eleanor was blamed. Rumours circulating at the time accused the Queen of poisoning her beautiful rival.

Eleanor bore Henry eight children. Family life, however, for the Plantagenets was not easy. All the sons quarrelled with their father, including his favourite, John. The final blow seems to have fallen when Eleanor was found to have plotted against Henry in support of Richard. For this she was imprisoned, her captivity lasting for fifteen years, only to be ended with Henry's death in 1189. During her time of imprison-

ment, Eleanor spent many hours working at her needlework, but although employed in this gentle art, she continually planned her husband's downfall.

Eleanor was a very strong women, influential in both political and cultural life. She gathered around her the finest poets, musicians and scholars of the age and founded educational and religious establishments both in France and in England.

On her release from captivity, she continued to spend her years in seclusion and after a long illness, at the tremendous age of eighty, Eleanor died in the Abbey of Fontrevault. The year was 1202.

## ⚜ MARRIAGE VOWS ⚜

The marriage ceremony of the Middle Ages was a relatively simple affair, usually performed at the door of the church. The banns were read three times, as they are now, and, assuming all was well, the following service was performed:

PRIEST     *Hast thou will to have this woman to thy wedded wife?*

GROOM     *Yes Sir.*

PRIEST     *May thou well find at thy best to love her and hold you to her and to no other to thy lives end?*

GROOM     *Yes Sir.*

PRIEST     *Then take her by your hand and say after me: I,…, take thee,…, in form of holy church, to my wedded wife, forsaking all other, holding me wholly to thee, in sickness and in health, in riches and in poverty, in well and in woe, till death us depart, and thereto I plight ye my troth.*

# ❖ A SHADY SPOT ❖

During the thirteenth century, English castles became much more homely. Good drainage became an essential requirement in better-class homes and walls were decorated with hangings to keep out draughts and to generally brighten up cold grey stone walls. Eleanor of Provence, wife of Henry III (who is said to have established the first public lavatory), and Eleanor of Castile, wife of Edward I, both shared an interest in gardening and particularly the growing of herbs. Eleanor of Castile even brought with her gardeners from Spain to provide her with some of the pleasures left behind in her homeland.

In order to enjoy the afternoon sunshine, a Plantagenet Queen might have sat out in a sheltered corner of her garden working a piece of embroidery. Romance was a favourite subject and apple blossom, violets, poppinjays (parrots) and fleur-de-lys were often worked on small cushions and curtains.

Arbours would have been made from banks upholstered with turves and carpeted with chamomile, bordered by a trellis on which would be trained sweet-smelling briar roses. Most seats in the garden would have been shaded by a construction of poles, tied with willow cords, often covered by vines or roses, as shade was essential to protect the precious white complexions of noble ladies. To have a skin tanned and golden was an indication of low status and thus of menial work.

Considering the unsanitary and noisy conditions prevailing at this time, even in the best of regulated homes, the garden must have been a little oasis of tranquillity and pleasure. Many of the plants grown were chosen for their perfume and would have included sweet violets, woodbine, lavender and bluebells – plants we associate today with an English cottage garden. The fact that many of these plants also had a medicinal use must have seemed an added blessing.

31

# ⊁ THE PERFECT GARDEN ⊁

*The garden should be adorned with roses and lilies, the turnsole or heliotrope, violets, and mandrake, there you should have parsley and cost, fennel, southernwood, coriander, sage, savery, hysop, mint, rue, ditanny, smallage, pellitory, lettuce, garden cress, and peonies. There should also be beds planted with onions, leeks, garlic, pumpkins, and shallots. The cucumber, the poppy, the daffodil, and the brank-ursine ought to be in a good garden. There should also be pottage herbs, such as beets, herb mercury, orach, sorrel and mallows.*

Alexander Neckham,
*De Naturis Rerum,*
thirteenth century

# ⊁ A PENNYROYAL LAWN ⊁

As we have seen, perfume was important to thirteenth-century gardeners and was skilfully used to delight royal patrons. Lawns of sweetly scented creeping thyme and pennyroyal were planted to release a gentle perfume as skirts and cloaks bruised their leaves. Pennyroyal was easily obtainable, it is said to have grown wild beside the road that ran from London to Colchester and was widely cultivated in the county of Essex.

Used medicinally, this low-growing herb was good for snakebites, gout and painful gums. It was believed to have a warm and penetrating effect and was widely recommended for chills, colds, bruises and even leprosy.

Pennyroyal can be used to pleasing effect in the modern garden. A sheltered corner could be planted with this delightful herb to produce an unusual lawn which needs no mowing – merely an occasional feeding and light weeding.

# ✠ THE STILLROOM ✠

The royal patronage of gardeners and interest in gardening led to the increased use of herbs in the stillroom. Mint was good for the digestion, whilst St John's wort gathered at dawn on St John's Day would cure sterility and produce offspring. Other unlikely remedies included peach kernels, bruised and boiled in vinegar, which were believed to cause the hair to grow upon bald places!

On a more useful domestic note, butcher's broom was used to scrub carving blocks (hence its name), and the ubiquitous herb 'mare's-tail' was employed to buff up pewter and to polish bowls and tankards. Pewter utensils were known as 'sadware' and unscrupulous tradesmen often passed off this inferior metal as 'silver' to their more gullible customers. Mare's-tail was also used by meticulous squires to polish up their lord's armour.

Dandelions were known to some as 'piss-a bed' and children for centuries have been told that gathering their flowers will cause an unfortunate nocturnal accident.

### A Good Dish for Health

Wash some dandelions and boil in salt and water. Cook until tender and hold under running water. Put back into a pan with fat, flour and stock. Stir until boiling and serve.

# ✠ A GOOD JUG OF ALE ✠

During the Middle Ages, most brewers and ale-sellers were, surprisingly, women. Most men who brewed treated the occupation as a part-time job. There were few inns serving ale. Buckets and jugs were usually taken to the brewer and the drink carried away to be consumed elsewhere. The more enterprising brewers often took their wares around the streets plying for trade, and on fair days stalls were set up for the refreshment of revellers. The quality of ale improved greatly in the fourteenth century with the introduction of hops and refined brewing techniques, and the town of Burton-upon-Trent became

famous for its ale. Home-brewed ale was often served at weddings and funerals, these occasions being just cause for drunken behaviour in most households.

The majority of the upper-class female population set great store by the frequent use of ale combined with herbs and spices which, being considered 'warming', were often featured in love potions to quicken the blood.

# ⚜THE ART OF COURTLY LOVE⚜

In Provence at the beginning of the twelfth century, poets began to write of a new kind of love. Born out of the feudal system of service, it usually centred upon a man caught in the snares of devotion, the object of this love being always a married lady of higher social status and, as such, to him totally unobtainable. To strive to be worthy of his loved one, a man must serve her without any question of reward. Although this new ideal originated in the south of France, it quickly spread through the courts of Europe and introduced a welcome new respect for women. Women had, hitherto, been considered the daughters of Eve, bearing the burden of guilt for Adam's expulsion from Paradise and, therefore, they surely deserved no consideration.

Well-born ladies naturally encouraged the new practice of courtly love and spent their time in intrigue and romance. Troubadours spent their days extolling the worth of a virtuous lady, and herbalists were employed to produce potions designed to heighten the senses.

*Beauty allied to great worth,*
*endless desire which daily grows*
*ever more tender and more sweet,*
*fond glances promising love, hope, joy,*
*tenderness and sweet satisfaction*
*make me love the fairest of all*
*ladies. So may God look kindly on me and,*
*in keeping with Love and her honour,*
*let me serve her like a true lover.*

Anon

## A Loving Cup

Put some toasted bread into a bowl and add 175g (6oz) of sugar and one lump of sugar saturated with orange-flower essence. Grate half a nutmeg and mix with the same quantity of cinnamon and ginger. Put into a bowl with 1 litre (2pts) of good ale and a bottle of mead.

## A Medieval Love Philtre

*25g (1oz) crushed cinnamon*
*25g (1oz) crushed ginger*
*7g (¼oz) crushed cloves*
*7g (¼oz) crushed vanilla*
*1kg (2lb) white sugar*
*1 litre (2pts) red burgundy*

Put all the ingredients into a large pan and heat slowly, stirring until the sugar dissolves. Strain and bottle.

Given secretly to the loved one, it was guaranteed to bring success!

# ⊁ UNWANTED VISITORS ⊁

On a far less romantic note, fleas and other vermin were a continuing nuisance, even in royal castles. A servant would have been employed, whose sole job it was to remove these troublesome insects from royal mattresses and clothing.

## A Fine Wholesome Ointment
### for the Bites of Fleas and Other Insects

Take 50g (2oz) of oil of scorpion, 25g (1oz) hedgehog grease, 25g (1oz) bear's grease, 275ml (½pt) of oil, 175g (6oz) red lead and 200g (7oz) white lead. Mix to a paste and lay upon a linen cloth. Apply to the bites, which will surely disappear. (Not recommended.)

*I hope there are no fleas, landlord, nor bugs nor other vermin!*

Question to be put by the traveller
seeking accommodation

# ⚔ LAVENDER AND ROSES ⚔

The scent of lavender and roses was greatly valued. The origin of today's 'potpourri' lies in the medieval 'sweet pots' used to perfume the somewhat noxious air of large manor houses and castles. The French word potpourri is used in preference to the English translation 'rotted pot', which sounds somewhat uninviting.

The original 'sweet pot' is also less attractive to look at than the modern variation, but it does last longer and gives a more subtle and indefinable perfume.

## *Lavender Faggots for Sweetening Linen*

*11 sprigs of lavender, freshly picked and pliable*
*1.5m (1²/3yd) 7mm (¹/4in) lavender or green satin-faced ribbon*

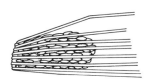

Tie the sprigs of lavender tightly just below the flower heads. Bend back the stalks, arranging them so that they form a cage (see diagram). Wind the ribbon in and out, pulling tightly as the flower heads are covered over. Tie firmly with a bow. Trim all the stalks evenly and tie again with ribbon, forming a bow for hanging.

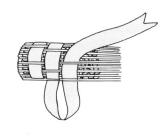

A set of twelve of these lavender 'batons' or 'faggots' was the traditional betrothal gift from her girl friends to a bride. Used to mark dozens and half-dozens of linen when packing a dowry chest, the lavender was effective against flies and moths. Lavender heads were also rubbed on the inside of oak blanket-chests as an insect repellant.

## *To Make a Sweet Pot*

On a dry summer day, preferably before noon, but after the dew has evaporated, pick a large quantity of perfumed rose petals. These must be spread on sheets of paper and left in an airy room to begin to dry. When picking the rose petals it is important to remember that they will lose half their bulk as they dry out.

After about 2 days, when the petals have become leathery, layer them in an earthenware crock or jar with 1 level cup of salt to 3 of tightly packed rose petals. The jar should be about one-third full. Transfer the crock to a dry, dark and airy place. Leave for 10 days.

Take out the crock and you will find that the petals have formed into a mass. Break this mass up and, to each 12 cups of rose petals, add the following ingredients:

*2 x 15ml tbsp (2 tbsp) ground cinnamon*
*2 x 15ml tbsp (2 tbsp) ground nutmeg*
*2 x 15ml tbsp (2 tbsp) ground cloves*
*4 x 15ml tbsp (4 tbsp) anise seed*
*100g (4oz) powdered orris root*
*50g (2oz) ground ginger*

Seal and store, shaking frequently. At the end of 6 weeks open the crock and add a few drops of oil of lavender, rose, jasmine (or indeed any combination which appeals). Reseal and leave for a further 2 weeks.

The sweet pot is now ready to transfer to pretty lidded containers. Keep covered at all times, except when in use.

# ⊹ THE SOLAR ⊹

The solar or withdrawing room was for the use of the lord and lady of the castle or manor house. It was here that they slept, entertained guests and enjoyed some privacy. Here too, in some cases, the ladies of the house would have spent their time spinning and weaving, producing

sheets, blankets and cloth for the entire household. The occupants of any large house lived in close proximity and even a Queen would seldom be left alone. At the end of the room would have stood a great open fireplace, from which the ashes were seldom cleared. The furniture of the time was heavy, hard and comfortless. Instead of wardrobes, chests were used to store clothes and precious possessions. The walls of the best solars would have been painted with stories of the saints in bright, often garish, colours.

There would probably have been a window seat and it was here that a lady might sit to work on her embroidery. It would have been a cold and draughty perch in winter as most windows were unglazed. Wooden shutters were used to keep out the worst of the weather, but these would also have blocked the light.

It is recorded that Edward II's daughter, Joanna, paid £2 7s 2d for gold thread, silk and pearls which were delivered to her chamber for 'divers works going on there, to do with them at her pleasure'.

Some much needed comfort was introduced to the wealthier homes when carpets were brought to England by Eleanor of Castile, wife of Edward I. Returning from the Holy Lands, crusading knights also brought with them beautiful and costly rugs.

Eleanor of Castile's modern habit of bathing was considered a strange custom. Previously considered weakening to the constitution, the Queen's innovation caused much speculation when a bath was installed in one of her palaces. Its presence indicated a sure sign of lewd behaviour!

# ⚜ PLANTAGENET EMBROIDERY ⚜
## *Wessex Embroidery*

This form of embroidery was practised from Anglo-Saxon times. It was worked in soft colours on linen to form borders and bands to decorate clothing and furnishings. Braids of Wessex embroidery were worked to add further decoration. The counted stitches employed were mainly simple, darning stitches being the most common.

## Underside Couching

This technique allowed the use of gold threads with no couching threads visible. The fabric on which it was used remained very pliable and the result was, indeed, very beautiful. As the couching thread runs on the wrong side of the fabric, the gold appears on the back of the work as tiny loops.

This method of using gold thread became extremely important, particularly in ecclesiastical embroidery. It was often used for both grounds and fillings and the stitches were often arranged in chevron and diaper patterns.

## Spangles

In the Middle Ages, clothes were often decorated with spangles of gold and silver cut into the shape of stars and moons, crescents and leaves. These spangles became a form of jewellery within an embroidery and often incorporated semi-precious stones and enamel work. They were often used in great numbers to enrich costly fabrics, in some cases forming the whole ground of a garment.

Garments were slowly becoming more and more outrageously decorated. Many students at Oxford apparently vied with each other to produce the most outstanding costumes, some going about dressed in 'gowns of blue satin full of eyelet holes, at every hole the needle hanging by a silk thread'.

## Wadded Quilting

*And she did sit upon his bed*
*A quylt ful nobil lay thereon*
*Richer saw he never none.*

Ywayne and Gawaine
fourteenth-century romance

Quilting arose originally as a means of holding several layers of material together to provide warmth, decoration and protection. A continuous filling of carded wool was sandwiched between two layers of linen or silk, and this would have been secured by decorative lines of stitchery.

It is widely assumed that the craft of quilting arrived in Britain with the returning crusaders. Originally a craft of the wealthy, their quilts were worked in costly fabrics in order to decorate their beds. The hangings that were displayed upon beds were, to the majority of owners, their most important possession, and many hours of work were needed to produce curtains of sufficient quality and importance.

In England, as the centuries progressed, quilting became the prerogative of the poor and the Mendips, Northumberland and Durham became centres of excellence. It was also to become a widespread craft in Wales and Ireland. As the popularity of these quilts increased, freelance quilters and markers toured the countryside, carrying with them their quilting frames. Markers were paid for the job, whilst stitchers were paid by the spool of thread.

Many regional patterns have evolved over the centuries, but the most functional and earliest is the use of simple diagonal lines. These show the natural texture of the fabric to excellent advantage, whilst holding the wadding securely in its place. From these basic lines, many groupings and arrangements were developed including squares, lozenges and wavy lines. In the North Country patterns such as the Weardale Wheel, Paisley Pear, Flat Iron and Heart have been used for centuries.

Early patterns were marked out by running a needle along the fabric, causing a light scratch mark, or by the traditional method of 'prick and pounce'. Today a water-soluble marker pen can be used, but care must be taken to keep the marked fabric out of sunlight or direct heat, as this can bake the dye into the thread, spoiling the finished embroidery.

*If a girl has not made a quilt by the time she is twenty-one,*
*no man will marry her.*

Old Devon saying

## A Simple Quilted Cushion

*2 x 40cm (16in) square of
fine linen OR cotton
1 x 40cm (16in) of medium-weight
cotton wadding
1 x 40cm (16in) square of calico OR other
backing material
spool of quilting thread OR
strong cotton or linen thread, well waxed
sewing needles (short sharps are best)
tapestry or square embroidery frame
water-soluble marking pen
30cm (12in) of Velcro or 6 strong press studs*

Trace the design from the diagram, and transfer to one square of linen, following maker's instructions on the marker pen.

Take this square of linen, the cotton wadding and the square of calico and pin together to form a sandwich. Stitch these together using long running stitches, starting from the centre and stitching outwards to form a cross. Then stitch around edges to secure wadding firmly in place. Secure this to the embroidery or tapestry frame and lightly stretch.

Thread a 'sharp' needle with a good length of single thread and begin to follow design in short running stitches. Starting and finishing threads should be run under the line to be worked. Never use knots or a double thread.

When the whole design has been completed, remove from the frame and, using the second square of linen, sew up on three sides to form a cushion (see diagram). Finish off with Velcro or press studs. Wash to remove marker pen.

## ⚜ THE KITCHEN ⚜

Interest in cookery was slowly increasing and during the Plantagenet age, the first cookery book was produced. Entitled *A Forme of Currye* it was dedicated to Richard II, the king who is also credited with inventing the first handkerchief!

A favourite dish of royalty at this time was the lamprey, a species of eel, called by the Plantagenets 'nine eyes' because it has seven little holes near its eyes. It was considered a great delicacy and it was partaking too freely of this dish that was said to have brought about the death of Henry I in 1135. Cooks were generally becoming more adventurous, and extending their repertoires to please their often difficult employers.

## A Fifteenth-century Doucet or Sweet Dish

*225g (8oz) shortcrust pastry*
*425ml (¾pt) double cream*
*pinch of saffron*
*2 x 15ml tsp (2tsp) clear honey*
*2 eggs plus 1 egg yolk*

Preheat the oven to 180°C (350°F), Gas Mark 4.

Line a 23cm (9in) flan ring with shortcrust pastry. Prick the base of the pastry case with a fork, line with foil or greaseproof paper and fill with ceramic baking beans or rice. Bake flan blind for 10 minutes. Remove foil or paper and beans or rice. Return to oven and bake for a further 10 minutes.

Put cream and saffron into a pan and bring slowly to the boil. Beat the honey and eggs together and mix in cream, continuing to beat well. Pour into pastry shell and bake at 180°C (350°F), Gas Mark 4 for 30 minutes until set.

## Lost Bread
### (Pain Perdu)

Dip slices of white bread in egg yolk, fry in butter until golden. Sprinkle with caster sugar and cinnamon and serve with lightly whipped double cream.

# MARGARET OF ANJOU
## *Wife of Henry VI*
### (1430-1482)

Margaret of Anjou was born in 1430, the daughter of René of Anjou and Isabel, Duchess of Lorraine. She was by all accounts a beautiful and intelligent child, remarkable for her age and times. It was because of her undoubted abilities that she was given a fine education, an unusual benefit for a Princess in the fifteenth century. As Margaret grew she displayed an interest in hunting, horseriding and many warlike spectacles. Embroidery and reading were to play only a small part in her future life.

As can be imagined, such a charming Princess inspired love and, despite her lack of dowry, many offers were made for her hand in marriage. However, a French knight imprisoned in London never ceased to regale his gaolers with news of her undoubted charms. This aroused the interest of the King, who asked to see a portrait of his cousin. Once seen, the King was smitten and vowed that this girl should share his throne. So, at the age of fifteen, Margaret was married to Henry VI of England. The political importance of this marriage was immense. England and France had been at war for 100 years and many English and French nobles rebelled at the thought of such an alliance.

Margaret's wedding took place at Nancy on 3 March 1445, with the Duke of Suffolk standing proxy for the King. Her wedding dress was of white satin, embroidered with silver and gold marguerites. These pretty daisies were featured everywhere, embroidered on cloaks, tapestries and banners. They were even scattered underfoot. However, after such a grand wedding, when the new Queen arrived in England, it was rumoured that she had brought no trousseau with her. Her entire wardrobe, including underwear, had to be paid for by the English.

During the reign of Henry VI, the rivalry between the houses of Lancaster and York, which led to the Wars of the Roses, came to a head. Friends of the Dukes of York and the Lancastrian Somerset are said to have argued in the Temple gardens. The dispute ended with the Yorkists picking as their emblem the white rose and Somerset's supporters picking the red. Margaret thereafter wore a red rose to show where her loyalties lay.

Margaret's life in England was surrounded with intrigue, violence and trouble. Her husband, Henry, was murdered in the Tower in May 1471, whilst Margaret herself was a prisoner in that bleak fortress. Her imprisonment there was to last for four and a half years, until Louis XI of France paid her ransom and returned her to her own country. There she died in poverty in August 1482.

Margaret's only son, Edward, Prince of Wales, died in 1471, and the death of the Yorkist Richard III at the Battle of Bosworth Field in 1485 led to the accession of Henry Tudor, the Lancastrian claimant, as Henry VII. His marriage to Elizabeth of York founded the Tudor dynasty and ended the Wars of the Roses.

## CHAPTER III

# The Tudors

And I will make thee beds of Roses
And a thousand fragrant poesies
A cap of flowers and a kirtle,
Imbroydred all with leaves of Mirtle.

A gowne made of the finest wooll
Which from our pretty Lambes we pull,
Fayre lined slippers for the cold;
With buckles of the purest gold.

A belt of straw and ivie buds,
With coral clasps and Amber studs,
And if these pleasures may thee move,
Come live with mee, and be my love.

The Sheepheards Swaines shall daunce and singe,
For thy delight each May-morning,
If these delights thy minde may move;
Then live with mee, and be my love.

Christopher Marlowe
'The Passionate Sheepheard to his Love',
(1564–1593)

46

# ELIZABETH I

*The Virgin Queen*
(1533–1603)

One of the dominant figures of Tudor England, Elizabeth was the daughter of Henry VIII and Anne Boleyn. She was born in 1533 and it is said that this birth of a girl child cost her ill-fated mother her head. A rumour popular during Elizabeth's girlhood was that this Princess was in reality a boy. This unlikely story hinged around the fact that the true Princess was said to have died as a result of an avoidable accident. Her nurses were terrified of the consequences of discovery – not really very surprising, when you look at accounts of Henry's temper – and so substituted a village child for their charge. In looking for another child, their main difficulty was the fact that Elizabeth was remarkable for her brightly coloured red hair. The substitute child had this feature but was, unfortunately, a boy! This story was often whispered behind closed doors as the true reason for the Queen's refusal to marry in later life.

As a girl, Elizabeth was taught to embroider. It is recorded that she made a gift of a cushion 'wrought by her own hand' to her governess. This cushion had, incorporated in its design, the initials ER in silk-and-wool tent and cross stitch. Although there is no evidence of Elizabeth sustaining a personal interest in needlework in maturity, she is well known to have loved rich and costly fabrics and embroidery. New Year's gifts to the Queen in 1578 included 'a veil with spangles and small bone [bobbin] lace of silver' and also 'a swete bag with small bone lace of gold'. Her palaces were perfumed and filled with herbs and flowers. In 1544, Elizabeth's New Year gift to her stepmother, Katharine Parr, was a book *The Mirroir or Glasse of the Synnefull Soule*, its cover worked with pansies, known to the Elizabethans as 'stepmothers'.

During her reign, bobbin lace became established in this country and Elizabeth was quick to appreciate the economic advantages of promoting the home industry. It was under her patronage that many of the Honiton and Bucks (Buckinghamshire) point techniques we still admire today were developed.

Elizabeth I *(by courtesy of the National Portrait Gallery, London)*

Elizabeth is said to have drunk beer 'so strong as there was no man able to drink it.'

At important banquets the first lady of the household carried in a roast peacock in his 'pride' (gilded and decorated with its own plumage). This centrepiece was followed by maidens all in white, and pages carrying the vast array of utensils needed to carve such a magnificent bird. Queen Elizabeth was once served a dish of roast peacock as she entertained the Duc d'Anjou. On this occasion the bird was presented on a silver platter, instead of the more acceptable golden dish. Elizabeth took this as a great personal slight, flying into an almighty tantrum and refusing to sanction the marriage of the lady who brought in the bird with the gentleman who carried the sauce. For nine long months the Queen refused to change her mind, as punishment for this gross misdemeanour.

Elizabeth became ill at the beginning of March 1603. Although her condition was serious she refused to take to her bed, but sat on cushions, reputedly sucking her thumb. On the morning of 24 March she passed peacefully away, ending the Tudor dynasty and making way for the Stuart James, son of Mary her life-long enemy. The England she left behind was, however, far more prosperous and settled than ever before.

## ⋇ DOMESTIC CONDITIONS ⋇

*. . . My house . . .*
*Is richly furnished with plate and gold. . .*
*My hangings all of Tyrian tapestry;*
*In ivory coffers I have stuff'd my crowns;*
*In cypress chests my arras counterpoints,*
*Costly apparel, tents and canopies,*
*Fine linen, Turkey cushions boss'd with pearl,*
*Valance of Venice gold in needlework,*
*Pewter and brass, and all things that belong*
*To house or housekeeping . . .*

William Shakespeare,
*The Taming of the Shrew*

The sweetly scented gillyflowers, so beloved by the Elizabethans, are known today as pinks and clove carnations. John Evelyn called these blooms 'July flowers'. Their name, however, is more likely a corruption of *girofle,* the French world for a 'clove', and aptly describes their sweet and spicy fragrance.

The first mention of the symbolic use of flowers was during the reign of 'Good Queen Bess' when the poet, William Hunnis, wrote, 'Gillyflowers for gentleness, marigolds for marriage'.

*. . .sweet flowers alone can say what*
*passion fears revealing.*

Thomas Hood

This idea was taken and developed over the centuries, to become almost a science in Victorian England.

Not only did flowers carry a meaning to those who took the trouble to learn it, they also contained powerful magic for healing and the finding of treasure. The humble forget-me-not was said to lead its admirer to vast quantities of buried gold and jewels, but only if it were pressed against the side of a mountain. The mountain then would crack open, leading to caverns of untold wealth.

To hold such beliefs seems strange today, but who has not told their child that there is a pot of gold at the end of the rainbow?

*The Spaniard eats, the German drinks, but the English exceed in both!*

Tudor saying

# ⚜ THE KITCHEN ⚜

Changes were taking place in the kitchen. Metal plates and spoons were replacing the earlier wooden ones. In some households brass pots were replacing those made of iron, but cooking was still done at the open grate with hooks for hanging pots and spits for roasting meats. Large houses would have been well equipped with their own dairy, bakehouse and brewing house, enabling them to produce all their own requirements efficiently and smoothly. In this period, English cookery was still dominated by the exotic spices of the East – ginger and pepper, cinnamon and cloves, nutmeg and mace. Meat was usually tough and often unpalatable. Spices helped stimulate the taste buds and improve the appetite.

Spiced drinks were fashionable and in early cookery books many recipes were given for caudles and possets. Their names conjure up a world very different to the one we know today. A posset was a soothing dish, made from bread and milk mixed with fortified wine; a caudle was a warming, nourishing beverage consisting of ale, well spiced and thickened with eggs. Do try this early recipe adapted from *A True Gentlewoman's Delight*, published in 1653. It is delicious and has such a charming name.

## The Countess of Kent's Caudle Cup

*500ml (1pt) of ale*
*yolks of 2 eggs*
*25g (1oz) sugar*
*¼ x 5ml tsp (¼tsp) mace*

Put the ale into a saucepan and bring to the boil. Remove the membrane from the egg yolks and beat them into the ale. Whip until the mixture thickens. Add the sugar and mace. Pour into glasses and serve.

## Elder Rob

*1½kg (3lb) freshly picked elderberries*
*350g (12oz) demerara sugar*
*½ x 5ml tsp (½tsp) cinnamon*
*½ x 5ml tsp (½tsp) ground cloves*

Put the washed and stemmed elderberries into an ovenproof dish and bake in a moderate oven until the juice runs. Strain through fine muslin. To each 550ml (1pt) of juice add 350g (12oz) demerara sugar, ½ x 5ml tsp (½tsp) cinnamon and ½ x 5ml tsp (½tsp) ground cloves. Put into a saucepan and simmer for 10 minutes until thick. Strain and bottle when quite cold.

The resulting syrup is said to be a cure for neuralgia and sciatica. Many spices were believed to be of medicinal benefit and this wonderfully named example survives as a cure for coughs and colds.

## Herb of the Sun

Amongst the spices well known to the Elizabethans, saffron must have been one of the most costly. From the crocus, *Crocus sativus*, only the stigmas are collected and it is said that over 200,000 are needed to produce just 500g (1lb).

Saffron was thought of as a herb of the sun and was taken internally as a cure for fainting fits and palpitations. In the area around Saffron Walden, Essex, field upon field was given over to its cultivation and, indeed, the town's arms depict three crocus flowers, an indication of the economic importance of saffron from early times.

It was fashionable, for many years, to dye household linen such as sheets, with saffron to give a yellow tinge. However, as hygiene was not of paramount importance to sixteenth-century housewives, dyed sheets were not laundered as frequently as white. They did not show the dirt! Someone eventually decided that this linen presented a health hazard, and Henry VIII passed a decree preventing its use.

The following recipe, to tempt Queen Elizabeth's appetite, shows the importance of just a small amount of precious saffron.

61

## Richmond Maids of Honour

*500g (1lb) puff pastry*
*200g (8oz) curd cheese*
*150g (6oz) softened cheese*
*4 egg yolks*
*150g (6oz) caster sugar*
*50g (2oz) fine white breadcrumbs*
*50g (2oz) ground almonds*
*nutmeg*
*pinch of saffron*
*juice of 1 lemon*
*grated zest of 2 lemons*

Heat oven to 200°C (400°F), Gas Mark 6. Roll out pastry and beat the yolks of eggs together with caster sugar until light and creamy. In a separate bowl cream the cheeses with the butter and mix in egg and sugar mixture. Beat in other ingredients and fill pastry shells. Bake for 10 minutes until well risen and golden.

These little tarts will rise beautifully in the oven. However, as they cool they will sink alarmingly. This is how they should be served. They are best eaten cold with, perhaps, a spoonful of whipped cream in the central hollow.

Elizabeth's mother, Anne Boleyn, was very partial to cheese cakes. These were baked, especially for her, at a cook shop in Richmond.

## Elizabethan Kisses

At all royal occasions it was the custom for the chief lady-in-waiting to carry a little dish of cakes to her sovereign and the chief guests. She handed them out with a 'faire cloth', on which they wiped their hands and mouths. Before serving the cakes, she would kiss the cloth as a token of fidelity and the little cakes, which were similar to meringues, became known as 'kisses' or 'tentations'.

## Michaelmas Goose

It was traditionally believed that Elizabeth was dining on roast goose on St Michael's Day, 28 September 1588, when news was brought to her of the defeat of the Spanish Armada. So overjoyed was she at the news that she commanded goose to be served each year at Michaelmas in honour of the victory.

# Queen Elizabeth's Christmas Banquet

1st Course

*Wheaten Flummery, Spinach or Stewed Broth*
*Gruel or Hotch Potch*

2nd Course

*Lampreys, Stock Fish, Sturgeon*
*with a side dish of Porpoises*

3rd Course

*Quaking Pudding, Black Pudding*
*Marrow Pudding and White Pudding*

4th Course

*Beef, Capons, Game, Mutton,*
*Marrow Pasties, Umble Pie★,*
*Scotch Collops, Wild Fowl*

5th Course

*Cheesecakes, Various Creams, Custards*
*Jellies and Junkets, Syllabub, Warden*
*Pies*

★Hence the expression 'to eat humble pie'. The 'umbles' were the sweetbreads, liver and lungs of an animal, especially a deer. These were stewed to form a tasty and filling dish, usually served to the more menial members of the household.

Catherine of Aragon
*(by courtesy of the
National Portrait
Gallery, London)*

64

# CATHERINE OF ARAGON
## (1485–1536)

Catherine was the daughter of King Ferdinand of Aragon. When she came to Britain as a child bride in 1501 to marry Prince Arthur, she brought with her garments and household linen decorated with blackwork. This no doubt reinforced its common name of Spanish work, used even though this style of embroidery had been practised for some time in England. Interest was nevertheless revived in blackwork by the appearance at court of Catherine and her ladies.

After Arthur's untimely death, Catherine was married to his brother, Henry, in 1509. Her inability to produce a living male child caused this marriage to be annulled in 1533, thus enabling Henry to marry Anne Boleyn. Catherine had refused to accept divorce meekly and for her stubbornness spent many years in isolation and imprisonment. During her captivity at Ampthill in Bedfordshire, the divorced and rejected queen is said to have spent many hours in lacemaking and embroidery. Thought of as a saint by local women, Queen Catherine became confused in their minds with Saint Catherine, the patron saint of lacemakers and spinners, and many stories and rhymes show evidence of this confusion. A bobbin lace stitch, known as 'Kat' stitch and still used today, is believed by some to have been so named because the Queen taught it to these Bedfordshire lacemakers to help them improve their livelihoods.

Catherine's interest in needlework lasted her lifetime, and at the time of her death in 1536 her household inventory listed sheets 'wroughte with Spanysshe worke of black silk upon the edges'. It is also interesting to note that Catherine's sister, Joanna (the Mad), spent many years locked away. When she died she left large quantities of drawn-work, embroidery and filet samplers.

Many stories are associated with Catherine, who had the love and respect of the ordinary people. There is a widely held belief that marmalade was invented by her servants. When the young Princess arrived in England, she longed for the fruits of her native Spain. Fresh oranges and lemons not being widely available, an enterprising cook

discovered a way of preserving the fruits for his mistress and marmalade has been popular ever since.

The explanation of the name, marmalade, however, is also said to have been connected with another royal lady. This time it is Mary, Queen of Scots. On her journey to Scotland from France, Mary was

laid low with seasickness or as the French say, mal de mer. Her women were distraught and offered their mistress a citrus preserve to soothe her. Its name was thereafter, marmalade, said to have come from the French words *Marie est malade,* 'Mary is sick'. A pretty story, but most unlikely!

## ✠ BLACKWORK ✠

Blackwork, often called Spanish work, reached the peak of its popularity between 1530 and 1630. It is thought to have originated in Arabia, from whence it travelled to Spain in the fourteenth century. In this work, black silk or linen thread was used to produce an all-over pattern of continuous scrolling. During the sixteenth century, designs ranged from tiny borders on cuffs and bodices to flamboyant extravaganzas enriched with gold thread, pearls and beads.

> *White was her smocke, embrouded all before*
> *And eke behynde, on her colar aboute,*
> *Of cole blacke sylke, within and eke without.*
> The Miller's Tale
> Geoffrey Chaucer (c1340–1400)

Confusingly, blackwork need not always be black. A few really early examples are worked in much lighter colours. And, when copying blackwork, it is well to remember that a true black pigment was not obtainable in Tudor times. It is necessary, therefore, to soften the black threads of today by the inclusion of a few strands of dark brown, blue or green. A more satisfactory alternative may be to experiment by dyeing

thread at home (see page 68). The limited number of simple stitches required to produce an attractive piece of embroidery make this an ideal medium for beginners. It is necessary only to combine dense patches with sparse areas to give a balanced design.

Today in order to work a piece of blackwork, evenweave linen is the most popular and practical choice. To produce a more authentic and traditional piece of blackwork a much softer fabric is needed, but to work successfully with this type of fabric requires a greater degree of skill. Always use a fairly fine ballpoint needle whilst working, to avoid moving and distorting the threads of the fabric.

## A Simple Blackwork Pincushion

In early Elizabethan times small pins were valued at less than 6d a thousand and large ones at 2s 6d. The pillows on which they were kept

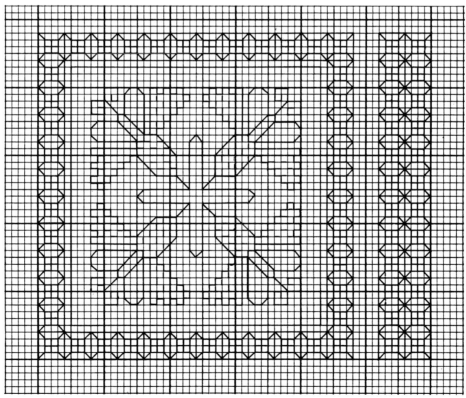

were often fine examples of the needlewoman's art. Pincushions were known as 'pin poppets' or 'pin cods' and were often given as gifts. In 1561, Elizabeth, herself received 'a cushion cloth with black silk and fringed with gold and purple silk, with pinpillow embrodred'.

*¼m (¼yd) of cream evenweave fabric*
*skein of black embroidery thread*
*scraps of dark green or blue or brown embroidery thread*
*fine ballpoint needle (the type used for sewing jersey fabrics)*
*small amount of kapok*

Using the evenweave fabric and one strand each of black and green, blue or brown embroidery threads★, work the panels as shown in the diagram. When all blocks of embroidery are completed, cut out carefully leaving a border of at least, 2.5cm (1in) around each piece.

Using a sewing machine, assemble the pincushion as shown, leaving one short seam unsewn. Using kapok, stuff firmly and evenly. Turn in last seam and catch stitch into place.

★If you have followed the instructions for dyeing your own thread, use one or two strands as required to achieve the best result.

The design for this pincushion has been adapted from a blackwork sampler worked by Jane Bostocke in 1598. This sampler, which is housed in the Victoria and Albert Museum, is believed to be the earliest dated piece of this type of work.

# *Vegetable Dyes*

If you would like to experiment by dyeing your own thread, the following method will give excellent results.

Choose a natural-fibre thread. Man-made fibres will not take vegetable dyes. Suitable threads would be of cotton, linen or wool. If possible buy an undyed thread, but if this is unobtainable white or cream will give the most satisfactory results. Do not be discouraged if your attempts are somewhat patchy, this will give a true reproduction of an early piece of blackwork and will be much more effective than using a commercially dyed skein of thread.

Most plant life will give some sort of colour. Sometimes different shades are obtained from the stem, roots or fruits of one particular plant, and these shades will also vary according to the time of year. It is,

therefore, necessary, to experiment until you find the required shade and it may be advisable to keep a record of the materials used, so that a favourite colour can be reproduced. However, as we are at the moment concerned with producing a dark thread for blackwork, the following list may be of help:

To obtain a black pigment use:
*Blackberries, Meadowsweet, Flag iris (root), Oak galls, Elder, Walnut bark*

To obtain a grey pigment try:
*Hawthorn berries, French marigold (flowers), Woody nightshade, Hypericum – St John's Wort, Yew bark, Broad beans, Blackberry, fruit and leaves, Privet, Dogrose hips, Willow leaves, Red cabbage*

To obtain purple pigment:
*Elderberries, Birch bark, Damsons, Bryony*

## To obtain dye from vegetable matter

Place the bruised or crushed plants in a large stainless steel pot and cover with cold water. Bring to the boil and simmer for half an hour. Allow to cool and strain through muslin into the dyebath.

# Mordants

To make the dye adhere to the threads it is necessary to employ a mordant, such as:

ALUM *potassium aluminium sulphate*
CHROME *bi-chromate of potash*
TIN *stannous chloride, muriate of tin*

## To mordant cotton thread with alum

*100g (4oz) cotton thread or fabric*
*25g (1oz) alum*
*7g (¼oz) washing soda*
*2 litres (½ gal) water*

Dissolve the alum and soda in the water. Tie the skein of thread loosely but securely with a length of cotton. Thoroughly wet the skein under a running tap and squeeze out all excess water. Add the cotton to the alum solution and bring to the boil. Simmer for 1 hour. Remove from heat and allow to cool overnight, leaving the cotton in to soak.

Next day remove the cotton, squeeze out all excess water and store rolled in a dry towel until required for dyeing. Do not rinse.

# Dyeing

Before dyeing the cotton, wet it thoroughly and squeeze out excess water. Bring the dyebath to the boil and simmer for 1 hour. Keep the cotton covered with the dye solution, adding fresh water if necessary. After 1 hour lift out cotton to check colour. Do remember that the dye will appear lighter as the cotton dries. So always dye a slightly darker colour than is required.

Silk thread can be dyed by the above method, but the results will be less certain.

Mary, Queen of Scots
*(by courtesy of the
National Portrait
Gallery, London)*

# MARY, QUEEN OF SCOTS
## (1542–1587)

Although a member of the House of Stuart, Mary is a central character in the story of Tudor England. Her rivalry with Elizabeth caused much intrigue and violence.

Mary was born at Linlithgow, West Lothian, in 1542. She was the only child of James V of Scotland and Mary of Guise. At only seven days old, her father having died, she became Queen of Scotland. As she lay in her crib, her nurse fancied she saw three crowns hovering over the head of her royal charge. This was taken to mean that Mary would, in later life, rule over three countries. One of these countries was inevitably thought to be England and this belief led, eventually, to Mary's downfall.

As a tiny child, she was betrothed to François, Dauphin of France, whom she married in 1558. On François' accession to the throne, Mary obtained her second crown. It was during her time at the French court that Mary began to take an interest in needlework. Her mother-in-law, Catherine de Medici, was interested in needlework and patronised many craftsmen and women. This interest was to be of great comfort to Mary in her future long years of captivity. François was never a strong man. He died in 1560, leaving Mary to endure her official mourning as his widow.

As soon as this tedious year was over, Mary returned to her own country. It was then she began an ill-fated relationship with her cousin, Henry Stewart, Lord Darnley. They married and she gave birth to a son, James. The marriage was a stormy one and suspicion fell on Mary when Darnley died in mysterious circumstances, following an explosion at his house at Kirk o' Field. More troubles followed for Mary and in 1567, after a tempestuous courtship, she married James Hepburn, Earl of Bothwell. This marriage was doomed from the outset and they were divorced amidst much speculation and gossip in 1570.

The Scottish Lords then rose against Mary. She was taken prisoner and banished to Lochleven Castle. It was there that she was deposed in favour of her son, James, who was made King in her stead. This must

# ✣ CHAPTER IV ✣

# The Stuarts

*Her work as fine as Queen Anne's lace,*
*That lines the country lanes in May,*
*Those skilled and work-worn hands embrace*
*Each spangled bobbin, bright and gay,*
*So deftly joined and finely wrought,*
*Plait and picot, bud and bride,*
*Flowers with thread and parchment caught,*
*Emblems of the countryside.*

Alice R. Elliott,
'The Old Lacemaker'

# QUEEN MARY II
## (1662–1694)

Mary Stuart was born at St James's Palace, London, on 30 April 1662, the daughter of the Duke of York (later James II) and Anne Hyde. Mary's mother came from an ordinary English family; she was, apparently, not beautiful, but had fine hands and arms and a good figure. As she got older, the Duchess of York gave way to the sin of gluttony. Her younger daughter, Anne, who much resembled her mother, was said to 'sup with her on chocolate and devour good things, till she grew as round as a ball'. Mary, however, in contrast, was slim and attractive in the Stuart way. She enjoyed riding, walking and dancing. One of her favourite occupations in later life was playing cards. This she did even on Sunday evenings, until criticised by the Church. Thereafter, Mary played cards whilst being read to from the Bible!

At the early age of fifteen, Mary was married (much against her will) to William, Prince of Orange. At the time of the ceremony she had known the bridegroom for just two weeks. After her marriage she was obliged to leave England with her new husband to take up residence in Holland. In comparison with life at the Stuart court, things must have seemed very dull. She is said to have spent much of her time walking in the woods around her home, or touring the countryside, her needlework upon her lap.

Meanwhile, in England, there was much speculation over the birth of a son to James's second wife, Mary of Modena. Rumours were rife that this child had been smuggled into the palace to be proclaimed heir to the English throne and, indeed, some even said that Mary had never been pregnant. This gossip reached Holland and caused a rift between Mary and her father which was never to be healed. England was unsettled. In 1688 the Glorious Revolution began and William landed to claim the British throne for Mary. James II fled and his daughter came home as Queen. Although Mary would have preferred to take the throne

Mary II, after William Wissing *(by courtesy of the National Portrait Gallery, London)*

herself, William insisted on his rightful place beside her and in 1689 they were proclaimed joint monarchs.

As Queen, Mary was the first member of the royal family to take a very personal interest in the welfare of her people, visiting hospitals and charities of all descriptions. This interest in the welfare of others probably sprang from the fact that William and Mary had no children.

In December 1694 Mary was taken very ill. On Christmas Day the disease was diagnosed as the dreaded smallpox. She died three days later, at the early age of thirty-two.

# QUEEN ANNE
## (1665-1714)

*One of the smallest people set
in a great place.*
Said of Queen Anne by Walter Bagehot

Queen Anne was born in 1665, the second daughter of James II and Anne Hyde. Her first suitor was Prince George of Hanover. His family, however, decided that as Anne's mother was a commoner George would be better matched elsewhere, so he went home to Germany and married his much more aristocratic cousin, Sophia Dorothea of Celle. After this bitter rejection, it was clear that a husband must be sought elsewhere for Anne and so, after a romantic and totally unsuitable, attachment to John Sheffield, Earl of Mulgrave, Anne was introduced to another George. This time, however, he was a Prince of Denmark. There were no objections to George as a prospective bridegroom. He apparently drank too much and was considered stupid by many; on the other hand, he found favour with Anne – he was blond and considered very good looking. This conventional couple were eventually married in a somewhat unconventional ceremony which took place at ten in the evening, after a trip to the theatre!

Despite her seemingly happy marriage, Anne never forgot her rejection by the Hanoverians and always, in later years, blocked any proposals that they should visit England. This was a rather short-sighted policy, in view of the fact that George of Hanover was to become King of England on Anne's death. Although constantly pregnant (she had eighteen pregnancies in all), Anne produced only one son who lived for any length of time. Much to his parents' distress, this boy died at the age of eleven.

On the death of her brother-in-law, William, in 1702, Anne became Queen, taking as her motto *semper eadem* ('always the same'). This motto had previously been used by her predecessor, Elizabeth I. Anne instructed that whenever her coat of arms was embroidered, this motto should be included. She herself had a great love of embroidery and spent much time in plying her needle. A panel in the Duchess of Wellington's

collection is said to have been worked by Queen Anne and shows Blenheim Palace. In the foreground is a scene of lovers surrounded by nymphs with flower garlands and little cupids. The jonquil, *Narcissus jonquilla*, was said to be the Queen's favourite flower. As she sat at her embroidery, she often wove patterns of this lovely bloom into tapestries, seat covers and dresses. Her love of this flower is reputed to have led her to establish the royal gardens at Kensington Palace.

At only thirty-seven, the year of her accession, Anne was already showing signs of obesity and gluttony, characteristics inherited from her mother. She suffered from continuous ill-health and so took little exercise. As the years passed, she became so ungainly that a chair was designed specially to lift her in and out of coaches and carriages. Despite her increasing size, Anne did, however, have beautiful hands and she used them to good effect when shuffling and dealing cards and when embroidering. Much time was taken up in writing letters to friends, the most important of whom was Sarah Churchill, Duchess of Marlborough. This friendship was to end in arguments and with much rancour but, at its height, the Queen referred to herself as Mrs Morley and to her friend as Mrs Freeman, in order to break down the class barrier between them and enable them to play the part of two middle-class housewives.

> *Queen Anne had a person and appearance not at all ungraceful, till she grew exceeding gross and corpulent. There was something of Majesty in her look, but mixed with a sullen and constant frown that plainly displayed a gloominess of soul and a cloudyness of disposition within.*
>
> Sarah Churchill, Duchess of Marlborough

One morning in July 1714, Anne rose as usual at seven o'clock and sat while her maid dressed her hair. Suddenly a lady-in-waiting noticed the Queen staring fixedly at the clock. Unable to speak, Anne collapsed and died forty-eight hours later. The golden age of Queen Anne had come to an end.

> 'Queen Anne's dead!'
>
> A popular response to stale news

# ⭑QUEEN ANNE'S LACE⭑

*Queen Anne, Queen Anne, she sat in the sun*
*Making of lace till the day was done.*
*She made it green, she made it white,*
*She made it of flowers and sunshine and light.*
*She fastened it to a stalk so fine,*
*She left it in the hedgerow to shine.*
*Queen Anne's Lace, Queen Anne's Lace,*
*You'll find it growing all over the place.*

Anon

Cow parsley is often called by the country name of Queen Anne's lace. It is not difficult to see how this plant came by its name. In May and June the hedgerows must have seemed, to lacemakers, decked out in yards and yards of frothy white lace, fit for a Queen. And, in fact, both Mary and Anne, in common with members of the nobility, shared a passion for lace. The wearing of this beautiful fabric not only enhanced the dress of those who wore it, but also made a statement of social position and affluence. The lacemakers were paid a pittance for their work, but lace commanded high prices. As with many other industries, unscrupulous middlemen took advantage of demand to make great profits and lace became a prized commodity.

Mary, in particular, exceeded all previous monarchs in her extravagance and addiction to this lovely material. In an account of 1694, rendered just before her death, her Mistress of the Robes recorded the enormous sum of £1,918 expended on lace for trimming garments and personal linen. There is also an entry for 21 yards of lace at £2 12s 0d a yard for trimming pillow cases. In the same account, Mary is said to have paid £17 for an apron trimmed with needlepoint lace. These aprons, worn by upper and middle class ladies were 'all the rage' towards the end of the seventeenth century. Highly decorative and very feminine, they enabled their wearers to play delicately and provocatively with sheer fabrics. The popularity of these items

declined, however, when Beau Nash, who detested such garments, ripped one from the waist of the Duchess of Queensberry declaring 'none but abigails [servants] wear white aprons'. The fact that this apron was of finest point lace and had cost 200 guineas seemed to him of little importance.

> *He scratch'd the maid, he stole the cream,*
> *He tore her best lac'd pinner.*
>> Matthew Prior, *The Widow and her Cat*

Those who wore lace during their lives often left instructions that they should be buried wearing their finest garments. In many families, a bride's wedding dress would be put away, layered with lavender against moths, only to be worn again at her burial.

> *No, let a charming chintz and Brussels lace*
> *Wrap my cold limbs and shade my lifeless face;*
> *One would not, sure, be frightful when one's dead.*
> *And, Betty, give this cheek a little red.*
>> Alexander Pope, *Moral Essays – Epistles to Cobham*

# ⚜ THE LANGUAGE OF THE FAN ⚜

The eighteenth century was the age of the fan. French artists such as Watteau and Boucher painted exquisite scenes on them and lacemakers were employed to make whole fan leaves of lace. The talented and artistic Princess Elizabeth, daughter of George III, is known to have painted a great number of fans.

The sticks and guards of these lovely accessories were fashioned from wood, ivory, mother-of-pearl, silver and even gold, and their display eventually took on a significance of its own. The messages a skilful and attractive woman could convey were said to wreak havoc on the most stern of masculine hearts. Indeed, even the exceedingly plain and plump Queen Charlotte, wife of George III, was reputed to have a beautifully shaped arm, which she was not averse to displaying.

*She had a fan in her hand. Lord! how she held that fan!*

Mrs Scott in a letter to her
sister-in-law, Mrs Robinson (1761)

So effective was the use of the fan in flirtation, that in Spain a whole code of movements was developed known as 'The Language of the Fan'. This became tremendously popular and soon spread through the courts of Europe. Placing the fan near the heart conveyed the sentiment 'you have won my heart', whilst pressing the half-opened fan to the lips must have maddened many an ardent suitor, for its message was clear – 'you may kiss me'. At the end of a romance, a fan placed behind the head with the little finger extended signalled 'goodbye', perhaps forever. The list of signs is endless and must have taken much practice to perfect. Schools were set up in order to instruct young ladies in the art, lest they should inadvertently convey the wrong impression.

Despite its seeming popularity, the language of the fan must have been, at best, a risky method of communicating and in Georgian times a sort of fan 'morse code' was invented. In this technique words were spelled out letter by letter, the ends of words being marked by an open fan. Known as The Original Fanology or The Ladies Conversation Fan, it was invented by Charles Francis Baldini and was published by William Cock in London in 1797. Even the simplest message would have taken some time to transmit and the system fell into disuse.

*Hither the heroes and the nymphs resort,*
*To taste awhile the pleasure of the Court,*
*In various talk th'instructive hours they passed,*
*Who gave the ball, or paid the visit last;*
*One speaks the glory of the British queen,*
*And one describes a charming Indian screen;*
*A third interprets motions, looks and eyes;*
*At every workd a reputation dies.*
*Snuff, or the fan, supply each pause of chat,*
*With singing, laughing, ogling, and all that.*

Alexander Pope, *The Rape of the Lock* (1712)

# ⚜ NEEDLECRAFTS ⚜

*For here's a Queen now thanks to God!*
*Who when she rides in coach abroad*
*Is always knotting threads.*
Sir Charles Sedley, *The Royal Knotter* (1707)

## Knotting

One of Queen Anne's favourite occupations was knotting, and this became a craze amongst the wealthy during the eighteenth century. It was worked with a shuttle, much like tatting today. Knotting was introduced from Holland in the seventeenth century and the shuttle was made from two oval blades, usually of bone, ivory, mother-of-pearl or tortoiseshell, joined together in the middle. This shuttle, which was held in the right hand, would be filled with thread and then passed through a loop on the left hand. The idea was to produce knots at regular intervals. This knotted thread was then couched on to a cloth, following a pre-drawn design. Knotting was used a great deal in home furnishing, usually on chair seats and bed hangings.

*I have been knotting all this day, in order to be a good workwoman*
*against you employ me. I wish you saw me work for I'm sure it*
*would make you laugh.*
Letter from Queen Anne to Sarah Churchill

## Stuart Embroidery or Jacobean Work

*I hardly could believe my eyes*
*To see hills, houses, steeples rise;*
*While crewel o'er the canvas drawn*
*Became a river or a lawn.*
Mrs Thomas Worlidge, *The Public Advertiser* (1766)

This type of work featured worsted or crewel embroidery in formal

floral scrolling arrangements on linen or cotton twill. It varied in scale from delicate borders to bed hangings heavy with stitchery.

The term 'crewel' is thought to be a corruption of 'clewel' work, taken from *clew* an old English word for a ball of thread. Hence, to work in crewels – to work in threads. Suitable materials included oatmeal cloth, crash or coloured cloth. Crewel-work stitches consisted of stem stitch or crewel stitch, satin stitch and french knots. Favourite inspirations for Stuart needlewomen were the Tree of Life, hills, birds and beasts – anything, in fact, to fill the space available. Although this embroidery had been popular for many years previously, by the seventeenth century it was universally employed. It is because of its undoubted popularity at this time that we still refer to this form of needlework as Stuart or Jacobean.

Wool colours were selected and graded so that pinks and reds or blues and greens predominated. Vegetable dyes were used, and these, when

A detail of a crewel-work hanging, part of a bed set *(Embroiderers' Guild Collection)*

subjected to light, suffer fading, so the soft colours we associate with this work today are not those originally employed.

> *Here followeth the certaine patterns of art workes, and but once printed before. Also sundry sorts of spots, as Flowers, Birds and Fishes, etc, and will fitly serve to be wrought, some with gould, some with silke, and some with crewell or other wise at your pleasure.*
>
> Richard Shorleyker, *The Schole House of the Needle* (1632)

## Boxers

In the seventeenth century, strange small figures appeared for the first time in needlework. These 'boxers', as they have become known, were portrayed nude, except for a fig leaf. Always shown with one foot in front of the other, they carried a trophy or palm raised in one hand. Often depicted as a repeating border pattern, they alternate with huge leafy trees.

Although the sudden appearance of these figures cannot be explained, one theory suggests that they are crude copies of Cupid. Another explanation is that they represent Daphne being pursued by the god Apollo. The modern term of 'boxer' is applied because of their curious stance, one fist uplifted, as if offering to fight.

As the seventeenth century progressed, teams of boxers formed border designs on samplers and blackwork embroidery. The modest needlewoman clothed them in little jerkins and drawers and sometimes even wigs, stockings and shoes.

## Hollie Point

This needlemade lace is characterized by its use of simple voided designs, traditionally made as an insertion. It consists of one stitch, a looped buttonhole worked over laid threads in successive rows. The stitch bears the same name as the lace.

87

It has been suggested that the name comes from the fact that the holes resemble holly berries. But 'hollie point' most probably comes from 'holy'. It was strongly associated with religious institutions and probably came originally from laces brought back by the Crusaders from the Holy Land. In Puritan times it was one of the few acceptable adornments to the dress, and was to remain popular for use on baby clothes until the nineteenth century.

Hollie point can also be seen in samplers of the eighteenth century. These were made by skilled adult needlewomen to illustrate motifs and techniques which could be employed to adorn articles of dress.

# ⚜ SAMPLERS ⚜

Early samplers were long thin strips of material, usually linen, which acted as a personal record of stitches and designs. Very gradually their purpose changed, and they became the teaching method for young girls learning to sew. The rows of stitching were the equivalent of writing practice in a first school book. As alphabets and numbers were most often seen on these early examples, it is possible that they were also used for more general education. In the middle of the seventeenth century it became common for the name and age of the worker to be added. The practice gained by working letters on these samplers would be of use in later life when personal and household linen needed to be marked with initials or monograms.

During the reign of William and Mary, a Dutch influence could be noticed in needlework, and samplers became squarer. Real Dutch samplers, although beautifully worked, tended to be of cumbersome and heavy design, but the English copies showed a lighter approach. Soon, these could be seen framed and hung on walls as pictures. Colours became brighter, and realistic flowers and animals were depicted. Vases of flowers, birds, pets of all sorts and even members of the family were portrayed, all arranged around a suitable verse. It was not until much later (the Victorian age) that religious sentiment and moral verse were considered the only suitable topics for this type of embroidery and the charm and naivety of the early samplers were lost.

Homespun linen was most often used for early samplers, although catgut is often mentioned, sometimes described as a coarse, sometimes a fine fabric, used variously as lining material or for handkerchiefs and gauze dresses. During the eighteenth century a form of bolting cloth was used for needlework, therefore frequently it became known as sampler cloth. This was an inferior grade of bolting or sifting cloth, originally produced for sifting flour. It was usually rather yellow and can be identified by the blue thread woven into the selvedges. Finer samplers were worked on a flimsy fabric known as tiffany; this showed silk threads to advantage and was often used by needlewomen to whom expense was no object.

The verse shown on the sampler illustrated here is taken from a harvest mug of around the end of the eighteenth century.

*Let the wealthy and great*
*Roll in splendour and state,*
*I envy them not I declare it!*
*I eat my own lamb*
*My own chickens and ham*
*I shear my own fleece and I wear it.*
*I have lawns, I have bowers*
*I have fruits, I have flowers*
*The lark is my Morning alarmer.*
*So my jolly boys now*
*Here's God speed the plough*
*Long life and success to the farmer!*

# *To Make a Stuart Sampler*

### MATERIALS
*Piece of linen, approximately 40 x 40cm*
*(15 x 15in), with a thread count of 22 per inch*
*Twilleys Lystra Stranded Embroidery Cotton*
✕ *2 skeins No 25 rust*
*1 skein of the following:*

| | | |
|---|---|---|
| ■ | *No 9 mid salmon pink* | *No 45 mid olive* ● |
| ▼ | *No 10 pale salmon pink* | *No 53 dark olive* ╲ |
| ◑ | *No 34 orange* | *No 78 light mauve* + |
| ✳ | *No 37 lemon* | *No 80 dark mauve* ◧ |
| ○ | *No 43 mid green* | *No 81 light purple* ▲ |
| ╱ | *No 44 dark green* | *No 82 dark purple* ◣ |

Use two strands of stranded cotton throughout.

Following the charted colour symbols, embroider the sampler in cross stitch. Finish by adding your own name and the date, worked in the space indicated.

### FINISHING
When finished, the sampler can be washed if necessary. Immerse the fabric flat in a bowl containing a biological, liquid detergent. Do not rub or squeeze, but sponge gently to remove dust. Leave to soak for a short time, then rinse thoroughly. Distilled water can be used for the final rinse to remove any trace of mineral deposits. Put the washed sampler on to clean towels and leave to dry, straightening it and smoothing it regularly. Avoid direct heat and strong sunlight. Once it is dry it can be gently ironed on the wrong side. Do not press too hard with the iron, as this will flatten the stitches and produce a matted look.

Using a piece of strong acid-free card of the correct size, stretch the sampler as shown in the diagram and mount in the usual way. It is a good idea to use extra strips of card between the mount and the frame, to prevent the glass from coming into contact with the fabric. Hang away from strong sunlight and avoid steam and condensation.

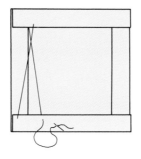 

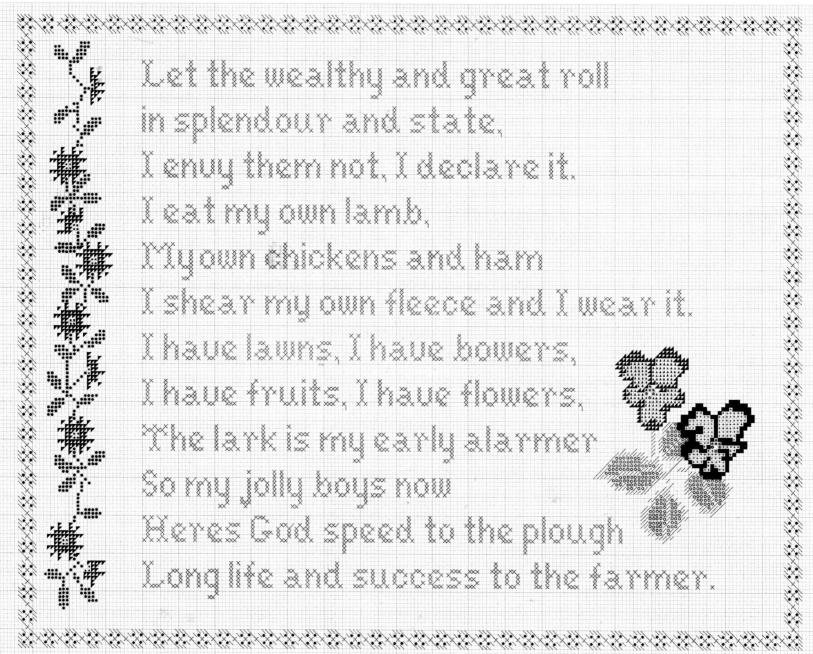

Let the wealthy and great roll
in splendour and state,
I envy them not, I declare it.
I eat my own lamb,
My own chickens and ham
I shear my own fleece and I wear it.
I have lawns, I have bowers,
I have fruits, I have flowers,
The lark is my early alarmer
So my jolly boys now
Heres God speed to the plough
Long life and success to the farmer.

# ⚜ COLOURS FROM A STUART WORKBOX ⚜

The following colours would have been available to the Stuart needlewoman, and although it is most unlikely that many of these names could be found on a modern shade card, it is interesting to read through them, with the possibility of matching them to those available today.

| | | | |
|---|---|---|---|
| ash grey | | lady blush | *pale pink* |
| beauty | | Lincoln green | *favoured by archers* |
| brazil | *red colour obtained from the wood of an East Indian tree* | marble | |
| | | medley | |
| Bristol red | *known since 1513* | milk and water | *bluish white* |
| cane colour | *yellowish tint* | plunket or blunket | *light blue* |
| carnation | *raw flesh* | popinjay | *green or blue* |
| Catherine pear | *russet red* | puke | *dull brown* |
| crane colour | | rat's colour | *dull grey, used for the funeral gowns of poor men* |
| gingerline | *reddish violet* | | |
| gooseturd | *yellowish green* | | |
| gosling | | sad | *any dark colour* |
| hair or maidenhair | *bright tan* | sheep's colour | *neutral* |
| | | watchet | *pale greenish yellow* |
| incarnate | *red* | whey | *pale whitish blue* |
| Isabelle | *greyish yellow* | willow | *light green* |

# ⚜ WASH DAY ⚜

The manufacture of soap began in London in 1524; before that date the trade was, apparently, carried out in Bristol. Queen Anne, obviously not concerned with the cleanliness of her subjects, put a duty of 3d a pound on soap and this tax was not repealed until 1853. The income from it at that time was reputedly some £1 million a year.

*For 'tis thump, thump, scrub, scrub;*
*Scald, scald away;*
*Oh, the deuce, a bit of comfort's here*
*Upon a washing day.*

George Cruickshank

In Stuart times, laundresses often suffered from bronchitis, rheumatism and internal complaints. The old-fashioned methods of washing were extremely unhealthy; steam from the boiling copper, long standing and heavy work combined with the sudden changes in temperature from overheated laundry to cold drying yard, caused a variety of chronic illnesses.

## Things to Remember on a Royal Washing Day

A vast army of servants would have been necessary to attend the needs of the Royal household. The washerwomen would have occupied a relatively lowly station in life, but their services were, nevertheless, essential.

The following basic advice, taken from a handwritten household manual, may seem obvious to today's housewives, but it was important information in Stuart times.

> *Soft water is better than hard. Hard water can be softened by boiling or exposing to the air. Rainwater can be saved. Tie a flannel over the top of the butt and the water will be cleaner when drawn.*
>
> *Soaking saves both soap and labour.*
>
> *Some people think it is very economical to wear things as long as possible before washing. This is really very extravagant, because linen allowed to become very dirty is:*
>
> > *unwholesome to wear*
> > *becomes of bad colour*
> > *needs more soap in the washing*
> > *takes longer to wash and so is the sooner worn out.*

94

# ⚜ THE QUEEN'S CLOSET ⚜

The brightly coloured embroideries and tapesties of the Stuart period must have been necessary antidotes to the gloom created by old, heavy oak furniture, low ceilings and ill-lit rooms. Amongst the greatest status-symbols of the wealthy Stuarts was the bed furniture – hangings decorated with elaborate and rich embroidery. Mary had, in her closet at Windsor, according to Celia Fiennes:

> . . . hangings, chaires, stooles and screen the same, all satten done in worsteads, beasts, birds, ymages and ffruits all wrought very ffinely by Queen Mary and her maids of honour.

Cotehele, the National Trust house near Saltash in Cornwall, has a suite of furniture which dates from around 1725. This suite is upholstered in a type of woolwork known as Queen Anne knobbed woolwork or Queen Anne's tatting. In this form of knotting, the wool is closely knotted before being couched down and is used for formal designs of flowers and foliage.

During Mary's reign, however, a more delicate style had found favour. Walnut became more popular for furniture and lighter fabrics were introduced. Chintz and printed calicos were used for dress and for furnishing. Mary developed a passion for porcelain and she made the collecting of it into a fashionable hobby. It was Mary, too, who started the fashion for lacquered furniture copied from the Chinese pieces imported by the Dutch East India Company.

> *The Queen [Mary] brought in the love of fine East-India Callicoes such as were then called Masslapatan, Chintes, Atlasses and fine painted Callicoes, which afterwards descended into the Humour of the Common People so much as to make them grievous to our Trade, and Ruining to our manufacture, so that the Parliament were obliged to make two Acts at several times to Restrain, and, at last, Prohibit the Use of them.*
>
> Daniel Defoe,
> *Tour Through Great Britain* (1722)

A walnut chair of 1690 from Cotehele House, Cornwall, with its original covers *(The National Trust Photographic Library/ John Bethell)*

In the homes of the well-to-do, the heavy furnishings of previous centuries were gradually being replaced with all that was light and clean. Elegant designers such as Chippendale, Hepplewhite and Sheraton were to appear to carry this new excitement forward.

The reign of Queen Anne also saw an upsurge in the middle-classes. These educated and fashionable citizens formed a sophisticated society, the like of which had never been seen before, and literary gatherings and musical evenings were held in drawing-rooms up and down the country.

# ❖ IN THE KITCHEN ❖

*Here thou, great Anna, whom three realms obey,*
*Dost sometimes counsel take – and sometimes tea.*

Alexander Pope,
*The Rape of the Lock* (1712)

Tea, which was then pronounced tay (to rhyme with obey), came to England from China via Holland. It was very expensive and in Sarah Churchill's accounts at Blenheim it is recorded that the Duchess bought tea for the Queen at £2 a pound.

It was somewhat unkindly rumoured that Queen Anne's dish did not always contain tea. Anne's nickname of 'Brandy Nan' gives a clue to the beverage the gossips implied the Queen favoured.

## *A Good Dish of Tea*
(1708)

Make 1 litre (2pts) of excellently brewed tea. Pour it out and set over the fire and beat therein the yolks of 4 eggs and 550ml (1pt) of white wine, a grated nutmeg and sugar to taste. Stir over the fire until very hot. Drink in china dishes.

## Queen Anne's Drinking Chocolate

*550ml (1pt) milk*
*1 stick cinnamon*
*3 green cardomoms*
*2 x 5ml tsp (2tsp) sugar*
*6 x 5ml tsp (6tsp) cocoa powder*
*double cream, whipped*

Put the milk into a saucepan with the cinnamon stick, crushed cardomoms and sugar. Heat gently until just below boiling point. Sprinkle in cocoa powder and whisk well over a low heat for 3 minutes. Strain and pour into cups. Float 1 x 15ml (1tbsp) of cream on each and sprinkle with a little extra cinnamon and cocoa powder.

Pampered Stuart ladies delighted in playing the 'milkmaid'. Dairies were turned into elegant rooms, where syllabub was served fresh from the cow and where wooden cows were available to dispense milk from their wooden udders.

## Queen Henrietta Maria's Morning Broth

*1½kg (3lb) boiling fowl*
*3 sprigs parsley*
*2 sprigs thyme*
*1 sprig spearmint*
*1 sprig lemon balm*
*1 Spanish onion*
*2 cloves*
*pepper and salt*

Put all the ingredients into a pan with enough water to cover. Bring slowly to the boil. Simmer for 2 hours, strain and drink broth each morning at ten.

Henrietta Maria was the wife of Charles I and it is recorded that she drank this broth every morning, without fail. She was excessively interested in her health and also enjoyed rose-leaf tea, a drink recommended for females only. Always delicate, she is reputed to have brought a more refined tone to English cookery.

## Lovage – A Drawing-room Drink

*25g (1oz) freshly gathered lovage seeds*
*½ litre (1pt) fine brandy*
*100g (4oz) brown sugar*

Bruise the seeds slightly using a pestle and mortar and add to a bottle of brandy. Tip in the sugar, put on cap securely and shake well. Put the bottle into a cool, dark place for at least 2 months, shaking occasionally. Pour the cordial through a filter paper. Re-bottle and use as required.

Lovage cordial was a refreshment much favoured during the reign of Queen Anne. It was drunk as an aperitif to stimulate the appetite and aid digestion.

# ✣ RULES FOR PRESERVING ✣ THE HEALTH OF THE BODY

*Never sit up late.*

*Never stay in bed late in the morning.*

*Sponge the entire body every morning with cold spring water. This should be done at once upon rising. Dry with a rough towel and continue to friction the skin of the whole person for not less than 15 minutes every day.*

*Drink four large ½pt tumblers of clear cold or very hot water each day upon an empty stomach. That is to say, upon rising, at 11am, at 2.30pm and at bedtime.*

*Take a corrective dose of medicine once each week.*

*Sleep with the window open at the top, even in wet or cold weather.*

*Keep the head cool by washing it frequently in cold water and avoid nervousness by resting often.*

# ⚜ THE VICE OF PAINTING ⚜

*Her mouth compar'd t'an Oysters with*
*A row of Pearl in't stead of Teeth;*
*Others make Posies of her Cheeks,*
*Where red and whitest Colours mix;*
*In which the Lilly, and the Rose,*
*For Indian Lake, and Ceruse goes.*
*The Sun and Moon by her bright Eyes*
*Eclips'd and darken'd in the Skies,*
*Are but Black-patches that she wears,*
*Cut into Suns and Moons and Stars.*

Samuel Butler,
*Hudibras*

Patches for the face are said to have been invented by the mistress of a French king, who wanted to hide an unsightly spot. She thus created a fashion 'look', which was copied in the courts of Europe.

Ever more outrageous shapes and sizes were invented, including the silhouette of a coach and horses designed to be pasted on the forehead or cheek-bone. To balance black or red dots, lips were coloured and cheeks too. So surely did this denote the path to hellfire to Puritans of the day, that in 1650 Parliament ordered an Act against 'the Vice of Painting and wearing Black Patches and immodest dresses of women'. As can be expected this Act had very little impact.

A sure way for a man to discover the extent of his beloved's artifice, was for him to eat a great quantity of garlic. He should then breathe heavily into his lady's face and the false colour would vanish quickly away – possibly taking the lady with it!

# ⚜ THE KING'S OR QUEEN'S EVIL ⚜

In Queen Anne's time it was still the practice for the sovereign to touch for the 'King's Evil', scrofula. It is recorded that in 1712 Anne touched Samuel Johnson when he was a toddler of only thirty months. However, the great man's companion, Boswell, observed that 'in this the Queen was ineffectual'. Johnson's complexion was badly marked as a result of this dreadful disease.

According to old medical encyclopedias the word 'scrofula' comes from Latin *scrofa,* 'a sow'. The condition manifests itself in the swelling of the glands of the neck and was thought to affect those of a tubercular constitution. It was believed for centuries that the touch of the sovereign could cure this ailment. In England this custom can be traced back to the time of Edward the Confessor and was probably brought over to England by the Normans, the Kings of France having 'touched for the evil' since the Dark Ages.

# ⚜ MANNERS FOR A YOUNG ⚜ LADY OF HIGH BIRTH

*Blush when modesty requires you to blush. It is becoming in a young female.*

*Forbear to speak loudly.*

*If it should be that a history of scandal unbecoming to maidenly ears be related or a joke be spoken, which is not seemly, be discreet. Drop your eyelids and give no impression that you have even heard of the same.*

*Be dignified in carriage and never affect languishing airs.*

*Control your appetite. Be not indelicate, be affable, be prudent and not a coquette.*

# ⊹A STUART PERFUME⊹

Lavender was one of the most popular perfumes of the Stuart period. It was used on all occasions and lavender water was said to be the favourite scent of Nell Gwynne, mistress of Charles II.

## *Lavender Scented Ink*

*15g (½oz) dried lavender flowers*
*8 x 15ml tbsp (8tbsp) water*
*1 small bottle lavender-coloured ink*

Crush the lavender flowers and put into a small saucepan with the water. Bring very slowly to the boil and simmer gently for about 15 minutes. Watch carefully and remove from the heat when there are about 2 x 15ml tbsp (2tbsp) of liquid left. Strain through muslin and squeeze out all liquid. Mix this perfumed liquid with the ink.

## *Lavender-scented Notepaper*

*box of lavender-coloured notepaper and envelopes*
*25g (1oz) dried lavender flowers*
*few drops lavender oil*

Put the lavender flowers into a small muslin bag and tie tightly with ribbon. Open the box of stationery and take out paper and envelopes. Sprinkle a few drops of oil into the box and leave to dry. Put the muslin bag into the box and replace stationary. Put on lid, cover the whole box with clingfilm and leave in a warm place for at least 3 months before opening.

# ❧ CHAPTER V ❧

# The Hanoverians

*What shall I do with the money I earn?*
*Up in the air it shall certainly turn*
*Soon as I hear the first cuckoo's 'cuck-oo';*
*Robin will hear it the same moment too.*

*Come, pleasant thoughts, and sit round in a ring;*
*Love is a cage in which happy birds sing;*
*So I will buy a new bobbin, I may*
*See one to suit me on Cherry Fair day.*

*What shall I do with the bobbin I buy?*
*Give it to Robin, for Robin is shy.*
*Then that I love him he plainly will see,*
*And he may buy a new bobbin for me.*

*Then in his arms he will clasp me and I*
*For him will live – though for him I could die.*
*What a sweet world is this! Now I have found*
*What it is – love it is – makes it go round.*

'The Bobbin Song',
from Thomas Wright's story
*The Lacemaker*

# SOPHIA DOROTHEA OF CELLE

*Wife of George Louis, Elector of Hanover*
(1666–1726)

Sophia Dorothea was married in 1682 to George of Hanover, who became George I of England in 1714 on the death of Queen Anne. Despite his inheritance, George always remained totally German, never even attempting to master the English tongue.

This first Hanoverian king of England was considered by many to be an unprepossessing man and the miserable Sophia Dorothea was sufficiently unhappy to embark upon an unwise affair with the gallant and suave Philip von Königsmarck. Their relationship was conducted in secret for some years before Philip's indiscreet boasting led to official scrutiny of their private correspondence. After a lovers' meeting at the Leine Palace in July 1694, von Königsmarck mysteriously disappeared. Papers were seized which implicated Sophia Dorothea, and the scandal broke. The King was advised to start divorce proceedings, and poor unfortunate Sophia Dorothea was eventually taken on 28 February 1695 to Ahlden, a small country town about thirty miles from Hanover, where she was to remain a captive until her death in 1726.

# CAROLINE OF ANSBACH

*Wife of George II*
(1683–1737)

Caroline was married to the future George II in 1705 and by all accounts they had a reasonably happy life together. Caroline gave birth to many children and, with her strong personality, it was believed that she ruled her husband and through him the country. The Hanoverians were not particularly popular with the people and gossip and speculation were rife. At one time it was popularly rumoured that Caroline was having

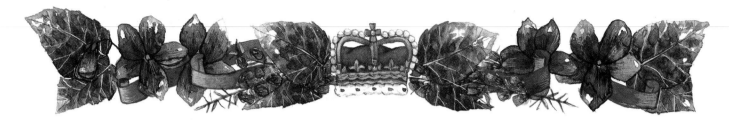

an affair with Sir Robert Walpole, as can be seen in the following anonymous rhyme:

*O may she always meet success*
*In every scheme and job,*
*And still continue to caress*
*That honest statesman Bob.*

Queen Caroline is also said to have spent her days in a less scandalous form of entertainment, however. She had a machine or 'engine' for knotting fringes of the type featured by Sheraton in his furniture design *Drawing Book* and she would, apparently, sit all day in old Kensington Palace innocently knotting fringes and gossiping to Lord Hervey.

The Queen also had a passion for polished furniture and the corridors of the palaces were said always to smell of beeswax.

## A Splendid Furniture Polish

Place 75g (3oz) of shredded beeswax, 25g (1oz) of white wax and 25g (1oz) soap in a clean jar, add 550ml (1pt) of hot water. Place in a warm oven, stirring occasionally until thoroughly mixed. Cool, bottle and store. It will be ready to use in 2 days.

When using, place a little on a flannel and rub into the furniture. Polish off with a silk handkerchief. Always keep in a well-corked bottle.

# PRINCESS AMELIA
*Daughter of George II*
(1711–1786)

Amelia never married and spent most of her life at home indulging in a variety of handicrafts. She was reputed to be extremely fond of knotting and there still exists a panel which may have been worked by the Princess with the Duchess of Newasch.

# CHARLOTTE OF MECKLENBURG-STRELITZ
*Wife of George III*
(1744–1818)

Charlotte was not a popular choice as wife of George III. Although of an affable nature, her manners were gross and she was often in desperate need of a bath. George, however, was initially well liked by his people. As a young man, he had a good appearance and high ideals. As he aged, his somewhat mundane approach to life earned him the nickname of 'Farmer George'. In later life, sadly, he was affected by mental illness, possibly porphyria, culminating in the incident when he introduced himself to an oak tree in Windsor Great Park in the mistaken belief that it was the King of Prussia.

Poor Charlotte's last years must have been extremely difficult. Her oldest son, the Prince Regent, caused scandal after scandal over women and gambling and her husband's ill-health must have been a severe trial. She died in 1818, just two years before her unhappy husband.

# PRINCESS ELIZABETH
*Daughter of George III*
(1770–1840)

Princess Elizabeth, the third daughter of George III, was very artistic and indulged in many forms of craft work. She possessed a box for filigree work made for her by Charles Elliott, furniture maker to her royal father. A grand affair, it was decorated with ebony mouldings, and lined throughout. With the box came 15 ounces of different filigree papers and an ounce of gold paper with which to finish the decorations. This filigree work consisted of narrow rolls of paper glued by one edge to a background of paper or silk-covered wood. Very fine examples of the craft resemble gold- and silver-wire filigree work.

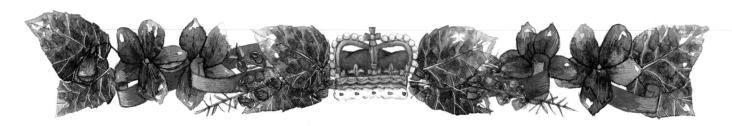

The art of paper-cutting reached its heyday in the mid-eighteenth century. One of its best known practitioners was Mary Delany, who probably taught the young Princess Elizabeth to cut paper pictures, and to perfect shadow perforations and pin-pricking. Mary Delany also invented the art of paper mosaics, in which flowers were cut from paper and mounted on thick drawing paper which had first been washed over with Indian ink. These pictures were greatly admired by Queen Charlotte and King George and some twenty of them are housed in the library at Windsor Castle.

Princess Elizabeth was also fascinated by the art of silhouette cutting and spent many hours making portraits of her parents and various religious and allegorical subjects. So involved was she with paper craft that the artist Henry Edridge painted the Princess seated at a window, happily engaged in her favourite hobby.

# CAROLINE OF BRUNSWICK
*Wife of George IV*
(1768–1821)

Caroline was not the wife the Prince Regent would have chosen for himself. 'Prinny', as he was affectionately known, was in severe financial difficulties arising from large gambling debts; his father's price for the settlement of these bills was that his son marry a suitable Princess. This turned out to be Caroline, thought by most people to be coarse, ill-mannered, dirty and fat.

The marriage, in 1795, was doomed from the outset and the couple remained together just long enough to produce a child, the ill-fated Princess Charlotte who was to die in childbirth at Claremont in 1817. So loathed was Caroline by her husband that he refused to include her in their coronation ceremony and the unfortunate Queen was locked out of Westminster Abbey, much to her subjects' amusement.

When the marriage completely broke down, George left Charlotte and returned to his liaison with Maria Fitzherbert, the lady with whom he had, in 1785, contracted a morganatic marriage. Maria must have spent much of her time awaiting the arrival of her flamboyant Prince

and she is thought to have occupied herself making felt flower pictures. A bouquet still survives, reputedly worked by Maria, which is composed of passion flowers, rose buds, auriculas and foliage.

Caroline, meanwhile, became more and more eccentric, even by the standards of the time. She adopted an odious boy, William Austen, allowing him to take all manner of liberties. At many dinner parties, the guests' digestion must have been severely upset by the sight of this awful child dangling over the table, snatching up sweetmeats and knocking over glasses of wine.

# ADELAIDE OF SAXE-MEININGEN
*Wife of William IV*
(1792–1849)

Adelaide was married to William IV, brother of George IV. It was her inability to produce children that led to Victoria's accession to the throne.

# QUEEN VICTORIA
(1819–1901)

Victoria was born on 24 May 1819 in Kensington Palace, the only child of the Duke and Duchess of Kent. She was christened Alexandrina Victoria.

Her grandfather, George III, was coming to the end of his long reign of sixty years. By now mad, blind, deaf and heartily disliked by his people, his duties were carried out by his eldest son, the Prince Regent. Prince George was, as a young man, a charismatic figure, full of fun and dash. However, the years were not kind to him and, as he aged, he became ridiculously fat and totally absurd. Although 'Prinny', as he

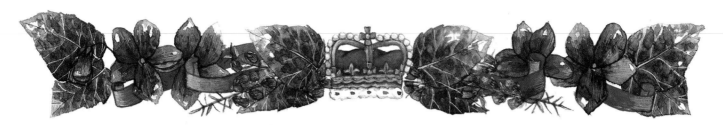

Model of Queen Victoria with her spinning wheel from Osborne House; she was also known to be fond of crochet and was photographed pursuing this restful craft on more than one occasion *(reproduced by gracious permission of Her Majesty The Queen)*

was called, had eleven brothers and sisters still living, none had been able to provide the old King with a grandchild to carry on the royal line. An unseemly scramble had taken place between the King's sons, to see who would be the first to produce a legal successor. This honour fell to Victoria's father, Edward, Duke of Kent, who had been unwillingly married to Victoria Maria Louisa of Saxe-Coburg-Saalfeld, a widow who had already proved fertile, having successfully borne two children.

Victoria's father died when she was only eight months old. It had become obvious that there would be no male child to replace her and so from an early age she was trained to be Queen. On the death of her uncle William IV (the original 'Silly Billy') in 1837, she ascended the throne. She was just eighteen.

The year before her accession was also an important one for the young Princess. Her seventeenth birthday was celebrated with a ball, given at Kensington Palace. Amongst the guests at this splendid occasion were two male cousins from Saxe-Coburg, one of whom was the handsome Albert. After the event, Victoria confided in her Uncle Leopold that

> *I am delighted with him in every way. He possesses every quality that could be desired to make me perfectly happy. He has besides the most pleasing and delightful exterior you can possibly see.*

Victoria married her Albert in 1840 and produced four sons and five daughters.

Although a determined woman, the Queen needed someone on whom to depend and throughout their married life Victoria leaned more and more heavily upon Albert's strength. His sudden death on the night of Saturday, 14 December 1861, left her devastated. She had every part of the room in which he died photographed, and ordered that his dressing gown and fresh clothes should be laid on his bed each evening and a jug of hot water placed on his wash-stand. His portrait was hung over her bed and almost every day fresh flowers were strewn on the pillow beneath it. The glass from which he had taken his last dose of medicine was kept on the bedside table, there to remain for forty years. Each night the grieving widow went to bed clutching his nightshirt.

In later years, Victoria was to find comfort in the friendship and care of John Brown, her Highland servant. He was a strong, outspoken man who was allowed to speak to the Queen with much familiarity, bidding her to 'drink up her tea' or to 'finish her lunch'. John Brown, however, was heartily disliked by the other members of the royal household, as a common and coarse character who had no place in the Queen's circle.

Throughout her long life Victoria enjoyed sketching and writing and, indeed, kept a journal from the age of thirteen until her death. Her sketches of her children are of excellent quality. Many subjects interested the royal artist, but she seems to have had little interest in flowers. The only two surviving flower pictures are a clump of heather drawn at her beloved Balmoral and a bunch of primroses, perhaps drawn in honour of Benjamin Disraeli whose favourite flowers they were.

Towards the end of her life, Victoria spent most of her time asleep in her chair. Then whilst at Osborne House on the Isle of Wight to celebrate Christmas 1900, she began to feel unhappy and unwell, apparently depressed by the cold and wintry weather. By 14 January she was unable to hold a pen in order to write in her diary – the first time in almost seventy years. Three days later she found it difficult to speak and her mind became confused. By the 18th it was apparent that the Queen was dying. Her children were sent for and the Kaiser hurried to England from Berlin. Victoria died on 22 January 1901 at the age of eighty-one, having reigned for sixty-three years. Her last word was 'Bertie'.

# ⚜ HANOVERIAN HANDICRAFTS ⚜

## *Crazy Patchwork*

A 'crazy' patchwork quilt dated 1860 is initialled VR and is believed to have been worked by Queen Victoria whilst at Osborne House. Distinct from patchwork made with shapes cut around a template, this method relies upon scraps of material joined together in a random arrangement, decorated with featherstitch. It became a favourite pastime in the nineteenth century, utilising silk and satin, velvet, ribbons and lace. As interest in the craft grew, all manner of 'objets trouvés' were incorporated into the designs, which were further personalised with mottoes, names and monograms.

Although the pieces seem to have been chosen at random, an artistic eye is called for to place colours and patterns in pleasing arrangement. Care should also be taken over the choice and weight of fabrics employed, so that individual pieces do not tear or stretch.

> *At your quilting maids, don't dally,*
> *Quilt quickly if you would marry,*
> *A maid who is quiltless at twenty-one*
> *Never shall greet her bridal sun!*
>
> Devon rhyme

According to tradition, a girl should make thirteen quilts for her dower chest. The last quilt made, which could contain a heart motif, would cover the bridal bed and was known as the 'marriage quilt'. This was worked by the girl without help from her friends.

## *Paper Fly Rests*

The Victorian era in particular is well known for its over-adornment of the home. Middle- and upper-class ladies with time on their hands found work of the most bizarre type to occupy their minds and fingers. In order to improve and beautify the house, ladies' journals suggested

the making of crépe paper wash-stand splashbacks and mobiles to be used as fly rests – it was believed that by providing these, flies would land and not buzz around the room. There was, it seems, no end to the ingenuity of these women.

## Pin-pricked Pictures

The raised effect of these pictures was produced by pin-pricking from the back of white, hand–made paper. Firstly the basic design was cut out and mounted. Simple motifs such as a branched tree or a garland were considered the most suitable subjects for this technique. When this main design had been completed exotic birds and animals were added, constructed from cut paper gummed into position and pin-pricked to give additional texture.

## Fisherton de la Mere Work

During the latter part of the nineteenth century, a free form of embroidery developed, inspired by the Arts and Crafts Movement and the interest of such eminent artists as William Morris and Edward Burne-Jones.

One of the many needlewomen inspired by this revived interest in high-quality embroidery was Mrs Arthur Newall, who in 1890 took on her first pupil. Mrs Newall's own work was strongly influenced by her love of Italian seventeenth- and eighteenth-century reticella needlelace and drawn thread embroidery. From this small beginning, Josephine Newall went on to establish a business, employing disabled and housebound workers, which was to continue for 30 years until her death in 1923.

The Newalls moved to the small village of Fisherton de la Mere in Scotland and from here a postal service was organised, sending commissions to outworkers and the finished work to customers. This business proved so popular, and the work produced was so fine, that this type of whitework embroidery soon became known as Fisherton de la Mere work, and it can be recognised by its flowing designs worked on fine natural or cream linen.

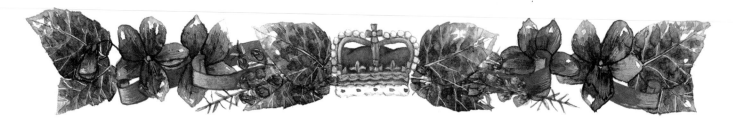

## Fish-scale Embroidery

Only the Victorians could have invented such a tedious and strange form of decoration. The scales of coarse fish such as perch, tench and carp, were used to produce floral sprays and exotic birds on fabrics such as silk, satin and velvet. The scales, which had previously been washed and separated, were arranged in curves or rounds, selected according to size and type. They were thought particularly useful to represent the delicate fronds of the maidenhair fern. In order to attach the scales to the fabric, a small hole had to be pierced in each one.

Fish-scale embroidery was obviously only suitable for items which were not to be washed, very much as sequins are used today.

## Orné Wool Work – Fluted Embroidery

This was a quite extraordinary method of embroidery. Pictures were built up using printed working threads. These threads were dyed in measured lengths, allowing for the number of stitches to be worked in each colour. Orné work was sold in kit form – the package contained wools, cord, canvas and a paper picture. The enclosed wool was also known as orné – a term applied to various dyed wools.

Lengths of dyed yarn were wound into small balls, sufficient to complete one horizontal row of stitchery across the picture. The canvas was marked with threads at regular intervals to assist the worker in maintaining the correct tension (which was vital) and thus produce an accurate design.

These kits were difficult to work correctly and very expensive to produce. It is not surprising, therefore, that the technique soon died out.

## Nacré or Mother-of-Pearl Work

Mother-of-pearl, probably the waste from button making, was trimmed into small shapes and sewn to such fabrics as velvet and silk. Embroidered details were often added.

In imitation of this work, stamped quillwork developed using opened-out birds' quills. This was called écaille work.

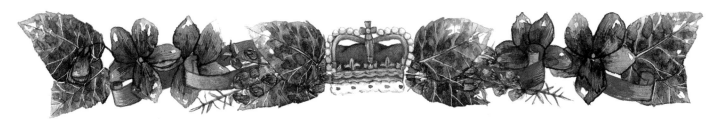

## Drizzling or Parfilage

The craze for drizzling which started after the Reformation reached its height in the nineteenth century. Metal thread from ecclesiastical embroideries and lace was unpicked and melted down for the scrap value of the gold and silver. During this madness, pearls and precious stones were also torn from vestments and church furnishings.

As the obsession with this pastime increased, tool cases known as 'drizzling boxes' were manufactured, containing tools and twin compartments for the gold and silver thread. Ladies and gentlemen would spend hours in this occupation, in order to earn a little 'pin money'. Social gatherings were arranged to enable the wealthy to 'drizzle' together, and indeed the Princess Charlotte owned a tortoiseshell drizzling box which was taken over by her husband, Prince Leopold, after her death. He apparently spent many afternoons drizzling in the company of his inamorata, Caroline Bauer, who complained to a friend that the Prince liked nothing better than to sit 'drizzling' while she read aloud to him from his favourite novels. The Prince was so industrious that he was able to buy his niece, Princess Victoria, a silver soup tureen with the money he earned.

The gold and silver embroideries of the Middle Ages were perfect materials for this dreadful craft, which might be found amusing were it not for the wanton destruction it entailed.

## Sea-shell Pictures

*I have got a new madness, I am running wild after shells. This morning I have set my little collection of shells in nice order in my cabinet, and they look so beautiful, that I must by some means enlarge my stock; the beauties of shells are as infinite as of flowers.*

Mary Delany,
1734

The talented Mary Delany, besides being adept at all forms of paper work, became obsessed by shell work and her work was commissioned by many members of the Hanoverian court. It included the making of shell frames for the Duchess of Portland's drawings. The Duchess introduced her protégée to the royal family. They were so impressed by Mary's talents that in 1785 George III gave her a house at Windsor and a pension of £300 a year. It is said that Queen Charlotte placed this sum of money into Mary's hands personally every year in order 'that it might escape the tax collector'.

Shell craft rapidly became almost a mania, which continued to blossom in the nineteenth century. It then became fashionable to create all manner of pictures with exotic shells. Travellers abroad were encouraged to bring back such shells, and kits were produced enabling valentines and greeting tokens to be produced at home.

## A Sailor's Valentine

*hexagonal or octagonal wooden frame*
*burgundy coloured mounting card*
*metal ruler*
*lead pencil*
*scalpel*
*an epoxy resin glue, such as Araldite*
*selection of small shells*
*a can of high-gloss clear spray varnish*
*a sheet of gold dry transfer lettering*
*small tin of clear satin matt varnish*
*small paint brush*

By searching the high and low tide marks on most British beaches it is possible to collect a good selection of suitable shells. When gathering your specimens, choose shells measuring 2.5cm (1in) across or less. The smaller the shells, the more attractive the finished picture will be. By carefully sifting the sand on good shell beaches, it is possible to find tiny microshells which are wonderful for filling in small spaces. Failing that, small beads can be used, but use ones made from mother-of-pearl, coral or polished stone for the best effect.

METHOD

1 Using the hardboard backing of the frame as a template, draw a hexagon or octagon on to the mounting board.

2 Place the card on a cutting board and, using the ruler as a guide, carefully cut

*Forget - me - not*

PEARS' SOAP

Established 1789

22 HIGHEST AWARDS
Gold Medal and Grand Prix

Pears' Soap is Guaranteed absolutely pure

out the shape using a scalpel fitted with a sharp blade.

3 Arrange the shells as suggested in the photograph, and mix a small quantity of glue following the manufacturer's instructions.

4 Start by glueing the centre shell in position and then work outwards, section by section. Leave each row to harden before applying the next and be sure to push each shell as close to its neighbours as possible. Keep checking the frame over the shell picture to ensure that there will be as few gaps as possible.

5 When the design is finished, leave to set for a few days. Then, following the maker's instructions, spray the shells lightly with high-gloss varnish. Leave for at least 30 minutes and then respray. Continue until a good finish is obtained (approximately four coats).

6 Leave to dry thoroughly before assembling the completed valentine. Using gold dry transfer lettering, apply a suitable motto to the frame and varnish carefully, using a matt satin varnish.

Shell valentines were peculiar to the Victorian and Stuart eras, in which all sorts of materials were used to produce decorative effects. Originally made by sailors for their lovers on shore, a pleasing picture can be made quite easily today, with the expenditure of a little thought and time, in the style of these lovely keepsakes.

All the shells would have been used in their natural colours, except for tellins or cockles which could be tinted pink or green to form the central rose and leaves.

# *Seaweed Albums*

Queen Victoria is known to have made a seaweed album for her mother, the Duchess of Kent, when she was fourteen years old. They were staying at the time on the Isle of Wight. These albums were usually composed of two large scallop shells joined together with ribbon, and into which sheets of paper were put containing strands of pressed seaweed. Even the best of these albums is fairly unattractive and reflects the less desirable side of the Victorian ability to produce something out of nothing.

*Call us not weeds, we are flowers of the sea,*
*For lovely and bright and gay tinted are we,*
*And quite independent of sunshine or showers;*
*Then call us not weeds, we are ocean's gay flowers.*

Traditional lines from
a seaweed picture

# ⊀ THE STILLROOM ⊁

### To Preserve Hair and Make it Grow Thick
(By the Queen's Tire Woman, 1760)

*1 litre (2pts) wine*
*handful of rosemary flowers*
*225g (8oz) honey*
*150ml (¹⁄4pt) sweet almond oil*

Mix all the above ingredients together. Pour into a bottle. Seal and shake well. Pour a little into the hand and rub on to the head. Comb the hair through.

## To Secure A Royal Night's Sleep

Queen Charlotte could not sleep soundly, apparently, unless it was upon pillows filled with the soothing scent of hops. Victorian gentlewomen, however, are said to have preferred the scent of lavender to calm the beating of their wildly fluttering hearts!

### A Sleep Pillow
### Fit for a Royal Bed

*plain white cotton pillow case*
*500g (1lb) dried hops*
*100g (4oz) dried sweet woodruff*
*100g (4oz) dried and crumbled lavender flowers*
*100g (4oz) southernwood*

Crush the herbs and mix well, then fill the pillow case. Machine stitch the open end and put on the bed in a pretty pillow case.

A recipe for the 'sleepless', recommended a herb pillow for those who by reason of 'great grief, much studying or long watchfulness cannot catch their sleep'.

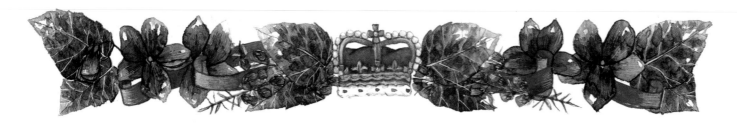

## Herb Cures

Medicinal remedies were still often quite bizarre, even in royal households. Queen Victoria advised a gargle made from cayenne pepper to cure a sore throat! And the following recipe, written by Princess Charlotte in 1815, shows that there was still a great belief in herbal preparations.

### How My Warts Were Cured

Take the bruised leaves of calendula officinalis [pot marigold] and blend with weak vinegar. (Paint on to the offending warts.)

## Cosmetics

For a special occasion, cosmetic needs could now be purchased from specialist shops which were springing up throughout London. An eighteenth-century shop which was famous for its perfume was The Sign of the Old Civet Cat. Here royal patrons could purchase special fragrances to use on state occasions.

# ⊀ THE DRAWING-ROOM ⊁

As she got older, Queen Victoria held 'Drawing-Rooms' in the afternoons. Lines of elegantly dressed ladies would wait for hours to be presented to the Queen in order to kiss her hand and perhaps receive a few moments of conversation. These occasions, as can be imagined, were extremely dull events, and in later years Queen Victoria passed the duty on to her daughter-in-law, Alexandra.

At four o'clock, Queen Victoria would retire to be served her favourite dish of marrow toast. For this simple dish, baked marrow bones were sprinkled with chopped parsley, wrapped in a napkin and sent to the table with pepper, salt and very thinly cut toast. The marrow was eaten from the bone with a long silver marrow-spoon. (It was surely not a suitable tea-time choice for her already over-plump Majesty.)

And on the subject of royal drawing-rooms, Lord Rosebery is said to have observed that he thought the drawing-room at Osborne the ugliest in the world, until he saw the one at Balmoral.

*The dullness of our evenings is a thing impossible to describe!*
Letter from the Queen's Maid-of-Honour 1849

## ⚜ HISTORICAL BOBBINS ⚜

Lacemaking was a thriving if ill-paid cottage industry throughout most of the Hanoverian years. It was not until the invention of the bobbin net machine in 1809 that the Industrial Revolution changed the lives of these poor women, making it impossible for them to continue to make even a scant living from their craft. In the 'good old days', lacemakers in their humble cottages would, with much pride, have recorded the events of royalty upon their pillows.

East Midland bobbins still survive with mottoes proclaiming 'Queen Caroline, died in 1821' or 'Queen Victoria, crowned 1838'. Famous victories were also recorded, along with milestones in the lives of famous men and women of the day.

On a more personal note, lacemakers would commission bobbins recording their own joys and sorrows. The heartache of a young girl of so many years ago is still apparent from the bobbin bearing the inscription 'It is hard to be sli[gh]ted by one as I love'. Men's affections must have been exceedingly fickle then, as this motto appears in almost every area in quite large numbers.

## ⚜ HAPPY BIRTHDAY, MA'AM ⚜

During Victoria's reign it was the custom to lay out birthday gifts on a specially prepared table. As can be seen in a watercolour by J. Roberts, Queen Victoria's birthday table of May 1861 was a particularly lavish affair. Amongst the gifts were clocks, lamps and many paintings. The whole room was decorated with an abundance of greenery and flowers, while above the table itself the initials VR were clearly picked out in wreaths of ivy.

# ✤ THE GARDEN ✤

With the Victorian passion for intrigue, gardens became places for clandestine meetings, with secret paths and hidden benches. These became favourite parts of the garden. Interest in exotic plants and flowers increased and specialist horticulturists vied with each other to produce bigger and more colourful strains of vegetables and flowers.

The interest in flowers, fruit and foliage spilled over into home decoration and articles abounded in ladies' magazines, advising on subject matter for embroidery of all types. In the list below taken from Miss Turner's *Crewel and Silk Embroidery* (1877), those marked ★ may be considered simple and easy to work. Miss Turner advised that:

*Considerable taste may be exercised in the proper choice of objects for the various articles to be ornamented. The bolder and more open foliages are required for such articles as sofa and chair backs; climbers and plants being capable of being designed in a running pattern for panels, curtain borders, etc; small and delicate flowers for mantel valances, bannerettes and other articles subjected to close inspections for this latter class nothing can be more beautiful than many of our too neglected field flowers, such as, for instance, the two flowered Linnoea, the Pasque Flower, the Hispid Mallow, the Germander Speedwell, and the charming ivy-leaved Bell Flower.*

*The colour of the surrounding furniture, with which the embroidery should harmonise, will also have to be taken into consideration when a selection is made from nature's varied stores.*

| | | | |
|---|---|---|---|
| Acacia | Dipladenia | Pitcher Plant | Sweet Pea |
| Anemone | ★Fuchsia | ★Pansy | Strawberry |
| Arbutus | Honeysuckle | ★Primrose | Sun Flower |
| Apple Blossom | ★Hawthorn | Passiflora | (conventional) |
| Begonia | Iris | Vermesina | Thorn (double- |
| Blackberry | ★Ivy | Passiflora (tacsonia | flowering) |
| Blue Flax | Jasmine | Buchanan) | Trumpet Flower |
| Clematis (Star | Mountain Ash | Pomegranate | ★Tea Plant |
| of India) | ★Narcissus | ★Poppy | ★Virginia Creeper |
| ★Corn Flower | Orange | ★Periwinkle | Vinca Major |
| Convolvulus | Peach (late | Rose (various) | Water Lily (with |
| ★Cherry (Winter) | Admirable) | Rhododendron | rushes) |
| Chrysanthemum | Primula (various) | Ragged Robin | |

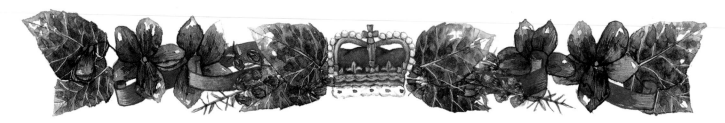

The following English dessert fruits are suggested for a set (one dozen) of linen d'oyleys, the apple and pear to be represented in leaf and blossom and some few others in blossom and fruit:

★Apple    ★Grape
Apricot    Peach
★Cherry    Pear
Currant    Plum
Fig    Raspberry
Filbert    Strawberry

# ⊹ IN THE KITCHEN ⊹

Before 1729, mustard was not to be found on English tables. In that year, according to Mrs Beeton, an old Durham woman known as as Mrs Clements discovered the secret of grinding mustard seeds. She apparently kept the secret to herself for many years, selling her mustard throughout the country. It was eventually introduced to the royal table, where it found favour with King George I.

## Durham Mustard

*2 x 5ml tsp (2tsp) mustard seeds*
*4 x 5ml tsp (4tsp) white wine vinegar*

Pour the vinegar on to the mustard seeds, cover and leave to soak for two weeks. Put into a mortar and grind until a paste is formed. Bottle and use as required.

## The 'Pudding King'

*When George in pudding-time came o'er*
*And moderate men looked big, sir*
*I turned a cat-in-pan once more*
*And so became a Whig, sir.*
       The Vicar of Bray

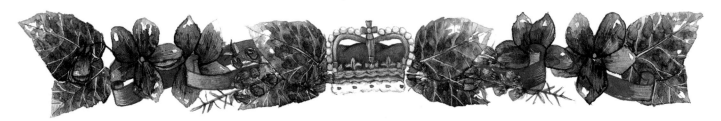

George I was known to his loyal subjects very disrespectfully as the 'Pudding King'. He was, it is said, most partial to boiled fruit puddings.

Queen Charlotte, the unhappy wife of George III, is said to have been completely addicted to all forms of pudding. Such was her reputation that many people believed that the dessert Apple Charlotte may have been named after her. However, a dish known as a 'charlet' appears in several manuscripts dating from the fifteenth century, making this theory unlikely. Queen Charlotte is also said to have been very economical, greatly disliking extravagance of any description. She was, however, very fond of mulberries and the trees growing at Buckingham Palace are believed to have been planted by her.

*Blessed be he that invented the pudding!*

Anon

## Queen Charlotte's Tart

*350g/12oz short crust pastry*
*juice and rind of 1 orange*
*juice and rind of 1 lemon*
*separated yolks and whites*
*of 3 standard eggs*
*50g/2oz caster sugar*
*150ml/¼pt water*
*2 x 15ml/2 level tbsp cornflour*

FOR MERINGUE TOPPING
*1 extra egg white*
*1 pinch of salt*
*250g/9oz caster sugar*
*1-2 tbsp granulated sugar*

Heat the oven to 200°C/400°F/Gas Mark 6.

Roll out the pastry and use to line an 18cm/8in flan tin. Prick base of pastry case well with a fork, line with greaseproof paper and weight with baking beans or rice. Bake for 15 minutes. Remove paper and beans and return to the oven for a further 15 minutes.

To make the filling, grate the zest from the orange and lemon and squeeze out juice. Put the cornflour, caster sugar and orange and lemon zest into a basin and mix to a smooth paste with a little of the cold water.

Put the rest of the water into a saucepan with the orange and lemon juice and heat until just below boiling point. Pour over

127

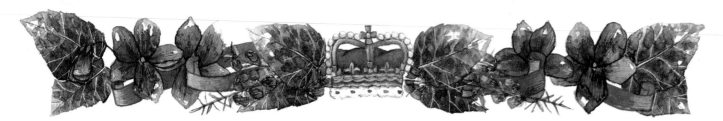

the paste, stirring well. Return to the pan and cook, stirring all the time, until the mixture thickens. Simmer gently for 5 minutes, stirring occasionally. Beat in the egg yolks and butter. Pour into the pastry case and leave to cool slightly.

Reduce the oven temperature to 150°C/300°F/Gas Mark 2.

Put the egg whites into a large bowl, add a pinch of salt and beat slowly until bubbles start to form. Now beat the egg whites until very stiff. Mix in 2 tbsp of caster sugar and beat well. Continue adding a little sugar at a time until the mixture is smooth and glossy. Pile the meringue mixture on to the tart, sprinkle with a little granulated sugar and return to the oven for 30-40 minutes or until pale golden brown.

*You may strut, dapper George, but 'twill all be in vain,*
*For we know 'tis Queen Caroline, not you who will reign,*
*You govern no more than Don Philip of Spain.*
*If you want all your subjects to kneel and adore you,*
*Lock up your fat spouse, as your Dad did before you!*

Popular Ballad
addressed to George II

## *The Chelsea Bun House*

As kitchen equipment slowly began to improve, baking became more fashionable and variations on the fruit bun began to be appear all over the country.

Caroline of Ansbach, wife of George II, was extremely partial to these particularly delicious buns and is said to have visited the famous Chelsea Bun House on many occasions. Such was the fame of this establishment that on one holiday weekend alone, they were said to have sold an amazing 250,000 buns.

*There's a charm in the sound*
*which nobody shuns*
*Of smoking hot, piping hot*
*Chelsea Buns!*

Eighteenth-century ballad

128

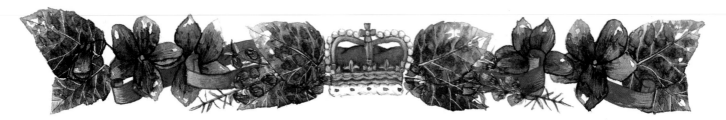

## Chelsea Buns

*500g (1lb) white flour*
*1g (¹/₂oz) yeast*
*225g (8oz) butter*
*225ml (¹/₂pt) milk*
*1 x 5ml tsp (1tsp) salt*
*2 x 15ml tbsp (2tbsp) sugar*
*2 eggs*
*1 x 5ml tsp (1tsp) ground cinnamon*
*1 x 5ml tsp (1tsp) grated lemon rind*
FILLING
*175g (6oz) currants*
*175g (6oz) brown sugar*
*175g (6oz) butter, melted*
*25g (1oz) caster sugar*
SUGAR GLAZE
*4 x 15ml tbsp (4tbsp) caster sugar*
*2 x 15ml tbsp (2tbsp) milk*
*sugar crystals (optional)*

Sift the flour and cinnamon into a bowl, add sugar and lemon rind, rub in butter. Mix the yeast to a paste with a little of the milk, add to dough with 2 beaten eggs and remaining milk. (It is not necessary to warm the milk except on very cold days; although using liquid at room temperature lengthens the rising period a little, it improves the texture of the dough.) Knead well until smooth. Cover with a damp cloth and leave to rise until double in size. Turn out on to a floured surface, cut in two and roll each piece out into a rectangle, about 25cm x 20cm (10in x 8in).

Mix together currants, brown sugar and melted butter and spread over two-thirds of each rectangle. Fold remaining third to middle and carefully fold other third over that. Roll out into a rectangle and roll up like a swiss roll. Damp edge with water and cut into slices 2.5cm (1in)

thick. Place on a buttered baking tray in rows, so that buns are almost touching. Sprinkle with caster sugar. Leave to rise until they touch and then bake in a hot oven 200°C (400°F), Gas Mark 6 for 20 minutes. Take from oven and brush with sugar glaze.

To make sugar glaze, put caster sugar and milk into a small saucepan over a medium heat and stir well until thick. Make this glaze just as the buns come out of the oven and brush each one well whilst still hot.

As an additional decoration, the hot buns can then be sprinkled with a few sugar crystals (the type used for sweetening coffee) as soon as they have been glazed.

A word of warning: Chelsea Buns are extremely delicious and rich in calories. They may have contributed to Caroline's weight problem!

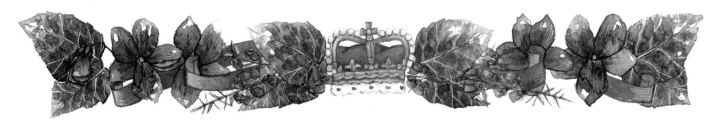

# ⚜ Queen Victoria's ⚜
# Christmas Dinner
Osborne – December 1895

*Purée of Celery à la Crème*
*Cream of Rice à l'Indienne*
*Purée of Pheasant à la Chasseur*
*Soles Frites*
*Sauce aux Anchois*
*Woodcocks à la Robert*
*Quenelles of Fowls à l'Essence*
*Salmis of Widgeon à la Bigarade*
*Border of Rice garnished with*
*a Purée of Pheasant*
*Filet de Boeuf*
*Roast Turkey à la Perigord*
*Roast Goose à l'Anglaise*
*Faisan – Gelinottes*

*Plum Pudding*
*Mince Pies à l'Anglaise*
*Pudding à la Gotha*
*Pudding de Cabinet*
*Nougats de Pommes*
*Tourte de Pommes à la Coburg*
*Gelée de Citron*

ON THE SIDEBOARD
*Boar's Head*
*Baron of Beef*
*Woodcock Pie*

WINES
*Sherry or Amontillado*
*Dry White wines*
*Champagne and Moselle*
*Burgundy and Bordeaux*
*Malmsey and Madeira*
*Liqueurs*
*Port, Sherry, Madeira and Claret*
*(Balmoral Whisky and*
*Apollinaris for the use of her*
*Majesty who takes nothing else)*

It is interesting to compare this with Elizabeth's banquet on page 63.

Queen Victoria kept a scrapbook of household hints and recipes. Roast beef and yorkshire pudding was a favourite for the royal main course. Victoria's aunt, Queen Adelaide, wife of William IV, is said to have been very partial to little dainty cakes named 'Queen Cakes' in her honour. It is very noticeable that all the Hanoverians seemed to have been more than a little preoccupied with their stomachs.

# ✦ CHAPTER IV ✦

# The House of Windsor

*Needlework as an art is as dead as the
proverbial door nail. The death knell
rang for all time when the sewing machine
was invented.*

Emily Leigh Lowes, 1908

# THE HOUSES OF SAXE-COBURG AND WINDSOR

King Edward VII, as the son of Victoria and Albert, was the first and only monarch of the House of Saxe-Coburg. His son George, who became George V, changed the name of this royal house to Windsor at the outbreak of war with Germany in 1914.

The two Queens featured in this chapter are Alexandra and Mary, sharing the same family, but of two different Houses, the former Saxe-Coburg, the latter Windsor.

# ALEXANDRA OF SCHLESWIG-HOLSTEIN-SONDERBERG-GLUCKSBURG
*Wife of Edward VII*
(1844–1925)

Alexandra was first suggested as a suitable bride for the outrageous Edward, Prince of Wales, at a dinner party held at Windsor on 9 November 1860. This party had been arranged for Edward's nineteenth birthday, but Bertie, as he was affectionately called, had not arrived home in time (from a tour of Canada and the United States) to attend the celebration. At this time Alexandra was only fifteen. She celebrated her sixteenth birthday a few weeks later on 1 December. This quiet Danish princess was strongly recommended to Victoria and Albert as a steadying influence for their eldest son. A naturally shy girl, she was unassuming and won the heart of most people who met her. In addition, she was tall and pretty, although in her early years the elegance she was to gain in maturity had not yet emerged.

As a child, Alexandra's upbringing had been sheltered. Her father, Prince Christian of Denmark, was a poor man by royal standards.

Married to the niece of King Christian VIII, his income and home were provided by the State. On King Christian's death, and the accession of Frederick VII, Alexandra's father was nominated heir to the throne and the family's living standards improved radically.

Reports of the young Princess found favour with Victoria and arrangements were made for the royal couple to meet. This meeting took place on the 24 September 1861 before the altar of St Bernard, in Speyer cathedral. It is said that Bertie was not over-impressed with Alix at the time, considering her nose to be too long and her forehead too high. However, on the 3 September 1862, Alix was taken to meet the now bereaved Victoria. Alexandra was advised that at this encounter she must on no account allow herself to smile and that she should dress plainly and simply.

> *Sea King' daughter as happy as fair*
> *Blissful bride of a blissful heir.*
>
> Alfred, Lord Tennyson,
> *A Welcome to Alexandra* (1863)

Victoria's impression of this meeting was that the young Princess was lovely, quiet and ladylike. It was on this occasion that Victoria gave Alix a sprig of white Scottish heather, picked by Albert himself at Balmoral.

Despite his misgivings, parental pressure was brought to bear on Bertie and, with the approval of the Queen, the wedding was arranged for 10 March 1863 at St George's Chapel, Windsor. For the occasion, Alexandra was dressed in silver tissue, a diamond diadem upon her head. As she floated up the aisle, her face was reported, by Charles Dickens, to be 'very pale, but full of awe and wonder'. After a moving ceremony, Alix changed into her going-away outfit of white silk with a lace shawl and white bonnet trimmed with orange flowers. An ermine mantle and muff kept out the frosty March air.

Alix was ecstatically happy with her prince. At the time of her marriage she wrote to Princess Victoria of Prussia: 'You may think I like marrying Bertie for his position, but if he were a cowboy, I would love him just the same.'

As a newly married woman Alix was in her element. She delighted in furnishing her own rooms with chintz and damask. Indeed she had the previously unknown luxury of a whole suite of rooms to herself in Marlborough House and these she filled with family photographs, scent bottles, trinkets and bric-à-brac. Every room was filled with the perfume of Alix's favourite flowers – roses, carnations and lily-of-the-valley.

*Queen Alexandra*

135

Not surprisingly, Alix soon found herself pregnant, her first child being due in March 1864. However, in January, whilst watching the skaters on Virginia Water, her labour began prematurely. After what must have been five hours of extreme panic, a tiny boy was born, weighing just 1.7kg (3lb 12oz). In the absence of baby clothes, Lady Macclesfield nobly surrendered her petticoats, and the baby, wrapped in these, spent his first night cradled in a nest of cotton wool. This child was to be christened Albert Victor Christian Edward, but would always be known to the whole family as Eddy.

In 1865 Alexandra's second son was born. This child was called George, despite his grandmother's objections. To appease the widowed Queen, however, Albert was added to the baby's list of names and he was duly christened George Frederick Ernest Albert.

As more children followed, Edward and Alexandra began to grow further apart. Ill-health had caused Alix to become deaf in one ear, and after a particularly severe illness she became lame and had to walk with a stick. Edward always craved excitement and this he found with a succession of women from various levels of society. The scandals and gossip caused by these liaisons were patiently borne by Alexandra. Indeed, many of his mistresses were actually entertained by the royal couple at Sandringham.

Alexandra found herself spending much time alone and she occupied herself with writing and needlework. She particularly enjoyed embroidery and would sit for many hours working at her frame. As girls in the Yellow Palace, Alexandra and her sister had frequently turned their hands to dressmaking and knitting in order to provide themselves with dresses and stockings. Indeed, once, whilst visiting an old woman in her cottage, Alexandra saw a sock being worked. She promptly sat herself down and busied herself with the knitting needles, as she chatted away happily.

On the death of Victoria in 1901, Edward and Alexandra became King and Queen. Alexandra was said to have been happier than she had been for many years. 'As Princess of Wales', she said, 'I was never permitted to do as I chose. Now I shall do as I like.' At Bertie's birthday procession of 1902, she was refused a place in the royal procession. Alix, as usual, made no complaint but, as soon as the royal carriage had left,

she ordered up her own and promptly tagged on behind as her husband moved off up the Mall.

As she aged, the Queen's unpunctuality became more marked. It had been nothing for the Princess of Wales to be twenty or thirty minutes late for a meal or engagement. Now this failing grew to irritating proportions. The difficulties in the marriage continued until the beginning of May 1910, when Bertie was taken ill. A series of heart attacks forced the King to his bed and he died just before midnight, his wife and surviving children around him.

Alix was sixty-five when Bertie died, although she always looked young for her age, elegant and beautiful. The years of her widowhood were spent mainly at Sandringham, where she often walked on the seashore and in the evenings worked on giant jigsaw puzzles or wrote increasingly rambling letters.

June 1912 marked the fiftieth anniversary of Queen Alexandra's arrival in England. This jubilee was celebrated by the inauguration of Alexandra Day, when millions of fabric wild 'Alexandra' roses were sold in the streets in aid of hospitals. Originally these roses were offered for sale by girls dressed in white, with sashes of scarlet – the Danish national colours. It is recorded, however, that Alexandra did not much relish this day, which always ended with her driving out in an open landau filled with roses. Not given to public appearances, the dowager Queen is said to have referred to the occasion as 'that tiresome Alexandra day'.

On 20 November 1925, following a heart attack, Alexandra died in her bedroom at Sandringham, sure that she was going to a reunion with Bertie, whom she had never ceased to love. She would have been eighty-one in December.

# * KNITTING *

Knitting is thought to have arrived in Britain before the fifteenth century. It is possible that soldiers fighting in France and Spain brought home this new skill. Hose or stockings, previously cut and shaped from woven cloth, came to be knitted. Indeed Elizabeth I caused quite a sensation when she appeared wearing 'fine black stockings' knitted for her in black silk by her silkwoman, Mrs Montague.

Over the centuries, interest in knitting of all types grew and thrived. The Victorians, particularly, busied themselves in the production of lace and beaded fabrics. By the Edwardian era, home knitting was flourishing and a wide variety of yarns and patterns was available. The garments produced by the Edwardian housewife tended, however, to be purely functional rather than fashionable, and the colours were often basic neutral shades.

With the outbreak of World War I, much emphasis was patriotically placed on knitting for 'our brave soldiers and sailors' – a sentiment echoed by our present Queen and her younger sister as they were encouraged to knit socks and mufflers for soldiers during World War II. This tradition of royal ladies taking up their needles and wool for the forces can be traced to Victoria, who is recorded as having knitted four scarves to be given to the four most distinguished soldiers serving in the Boer War (1899–1902).

There was, however, a lighter side to this craft, as can be seen from this pattern adapted from a leaflet produced in the 1930s.

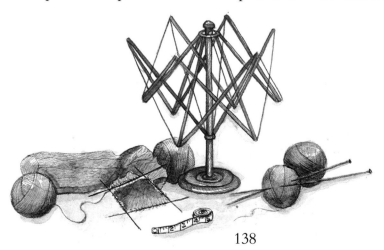

# Lace Mittens

*2 x 20g balls of Twilleys Crochet Cotton No 20*
*1 pair 2¼mm (No 13) knitting needles*

TENSION Over main pattern, 8 sts and 14 rows to 25mm (1in)

ABBREVIATIONS k, knit; p, purl; st, stitch; sts, stitches; rep, repeat; tog, together; yfd, yarn forward; yrn, yarn round needle; sl, slip; psso, pass slip stitch over.

RIGHT MITTEN

*Cuff*

Cast on 19 sts.

1st row: K3, yfd, k2tog, k5, (yfd, k2tog) twice, k1, p1, k2tog, k1 (18 sts)

2nd and every following alternate row: Make 1 st putting yrn before knitting first st, then k2tog, k to last 3 sts, yfd, k2tog, k1

3rd row: K3, yfd, k2tog, k3, k2tog, (yfd, k2tog) twice, (k1, yfd) twice, k2 (19 sts)

5th row: K3, yfd, k2tog, k2, k2tog, (yfd, k2tog) twice, k1, yfd, k3, yfd, k2 (20 sts)

7th row: K3, yfd, k2tog, k1, k2tog, (yfd k2tog) twice, k1, yfd, k5, yfd, k2 (21 sts)

9th row: K3, yfd, (k2tog) twice, (yfd, k2tog) twice, k1, yfd, k7, yfd, k2 (22 sts)

11th row: K3, yfd, k2tog, k2, (yfd, k2tog) twice, k1, yfd, k2tog, k3, k2tog, yfd, k2tog, k1 (21 sts)

13th row: K3, yfd, k2tog, k3, (yfd, k2tog) twice, k1, yfd, k2tog, k1, k2tog, yfd, k2tog, k1 (20 sts)

15th row: K3, yfd, k2tog, k4, (yfd, k2tog) twice, k1, yfd, sl1, k2tog, psso, yfd, k2tog, k1 (19 sts)

16th row: As 2nd row

These 16 rows form the pattern. Rep 9 times in all, then rep 1st to 15th rows once more. Cast off. Do not break yarn, but with right side of work facing, pick up and k79 sts along straight edge of cuff.

*Hand section*

Next row: On wrong side of work (p1, p2tog, p2, p2tog) to last 2 sts, p2tog (56 sts)

Work 6 rows in k1, p1 rib

Begin main pattern:

1st row: K1, (yfd k2tog) to last st, k1

2nd row: P1, (yrn, p2tog) to last st, k1

Repeat these 2 rows 15 times more

Now shape thumb as follows:

1st row: K1, (yfd, k2tog) 19 times, turn, leaving remaining 17 sts on a spare needle

2nd row: Cast on 9 sts, then p1, (yrn, p2tog) 10 times, turn, leaving remaining 27 sts on 2nd needle

Cast on 9 sts (30 sts on needle)

3rd row: As 2nd main pattern row

4th row: K3tog, (yfd, k2tog) 12 times, k3tog

5th row: As 2nd row

Rep 1st and 2nd main pattern rows once

8th row: K3tog, (yfd, k2tog) 10 times, k3tog

9th row: As 2nd row

Rep 1st and 2nd rows 6 times

Cast off fairly firmly

Break yarn, thread it through a darning needle and sew up thumb seam

With right side of work facing, pick up

and k 16 sts along cast-on edge of thumb. Then work over the 17 sts on first spare needle as follows: (yrn, k2tog) 8 times, k1
Next row: P1 (yrn, p2tog) 16 times, then work across the 27 sts on second spare needle thus: (yrn p2tog) 13 times, p1
Repeat 1st and 2nd rows once
Next row: K1, (yrn, k2tog) 13 times, k3tog, k1, (yfd, k2tog) 4 times, k1, k3tog, (yfd, k2tog) 8 times, k1
Repeat 2nd row once, then rep 1st and 2nd rows once more
Next row: K1, (yfd, k2tog) 13 times, k3tog, k1, (yfd, k2tog) twice, k1, k3tog, (yfd, k2tog) 8 times, k1
Next row: As 2nd row
Now work 1st and 2nd rows 7 times before commencing fingers, as follows:

*1st finger*
1st row: K1 (yfd, k2tog) 16 times, k1, turn, leaving rem sts on a spare needle
2nd row: Cast on 2 sts, p1 (yrn, p2tog) 8 times, p1, turn, leaving rem sts on a second spare needle
3rd row: Cast on 2 sts (20 sts) and work 1st main pattern row
4th row: As 2nd pattern row
Repeat 1st and 2nd pattern rows 8 times more.
Cast off fairly firmly and sew up seam as for thumb.

*2nd finger*
1st row: Join on yarn and, with right side facing, pick up and k 4 sts from those cast on at base of preceding finger. Work over 6 sts from 1st spare needle thus: k1, (yfd, k2tog) twice, k1, turn

2nd row: Cast on 2 sts (12 sts) then work over these 12 sts and 6 sts from inner end of 2nd needle thus: p1, (yrn, p2tog) 8 times, p1, turn
3rd row: Cast on 2 sts, (20 sts) and work as for 1st pattern row
4th row: As 2nd pattern row
Repeat 1st and 2nd pattern rows, 10 times more.
Cast off and sew up seam as before.

*3rd finger*
Work as for 2nd finger, but repeat 1st and 2nd pattern rows only 8 times.

*4th finger*
1st row: With right side facing, pick up and k 4 sts from base of the 3rd finger, then work over remaining 6 sts on 1st spare needle thus: k1, (yfd, k2tog) twice, k1. Now work over these 10 sts and the last 6 sts taken from 2nd spare needle as follows:
Next row: P1, (yrn, p2tog) to last st, p1. Repeat 1st and 2nd pattern rows 6 times. Cast off as before. Sew up side seam of glove.

LEFT MITTEN
Work as right mitten until shaping for thumb is reached:
1st row: K1, (yfd, k2tog) 14 times, turn, leaving remaining 27 sts on spare needle
2nd row: Cast on 9 sts, then p1, (yrn, p2tog) 10 times, turn, leaving remaining 17 sts on 2nd spare needle.
Now work as for thumb of right mitten.
Then complete, following instructions for right mitten, reversing the instructions where necessary.

# ✦ FILET CROCHET ✦

Edwardian crochet patterns were copied from earlier filet lace, which can be traced back in its origins to the fourteenth-century 'opus filatorium', or darned net. In that technique a squared 'net' mesh was first worked, upon which various embroidered decorations were applied. Filet crochet produces a similar fabric, but both net and design are worked simultaneously. During the Victorian and Edwardian period this type of work was most often seen on household linen, particularly as an edging on sheets, pillowcases and table-cloths.

## *A Filet Crochet Edging*
### *(sufficient to edge a single sheet)*

*3 x 20g balls Twilleys crochet cotton No 20 in white*
*1.50 (no 2½) crochet hook*
*2m (2¼yd) single-faced 7mm (¼in) white satin ribbon*

Begin by making 67 chain. Then work a foundation row as follows:

Make a double treble into the 4th chain from hook. Continue by making a further 2 double trebles into the next 2 chain stitches – a block of 4 double trebles has thus been worked. Work 2 chain followed by a double treble into the 3rd chain★ (a space has thus been worked) ★ repeat until 17 spaces have been worked. Make 4 double trebles into the next 4 chain, work 1 space, followed by 4 double trebles.

Turn work and increase as shown in small diagram. Continue following the chart, increasing and decreasing as shown on the outer edge. To increase on 2nd and every following even row work 6 turning chains (2 forming the base of a new mesh and 4 to form first double treble of next row). Then work 2 double trebles into this chain and 1 into the last double treble of the previous row. To increase on 3rd and every following odd row work 1 double treble into same st as last double treble (work 1 double treble into base of last double treble) twice, turn.

Continue until work fits edge of sheet. Using a safety pin, thread ribbon through holes on inner edge of crochet. Finish off and sew in ends. Press lightly and sew neatly to edge of sheet. Starch sheet lightly and press.

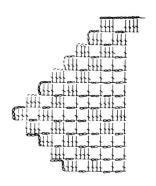

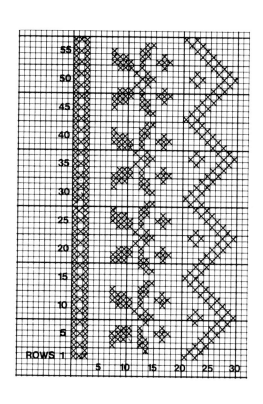

142

# ⚜A Dainty Dish to Set⚜ Before the Queen

King Edward is known to have heartily enjoyed robust food in vast quantities. Indeed, at bedtime a dish of cold roast chicken was often placed on a side-table in his room in case his Royal Majesty should feel peckish during the night. On the other hand, his wife ate much more sparingly and her favourite dish was said to be supreme of chicken.

## Chicken Supreme Alexandra
### (serves 4)

A supreme of chicken is the boned and skinned breast of the chicken. It is always used in the most elegant, pan-fried dishes and the following method of preparation was a great favourite of Queen Alexandra.

*2 plump roasting chickens 1½-1¾kg (3-4lb) each*
*salt and freshly ground black pepper*
*50g (2oz) clarified butter*
*150ml (¼pt) good strong chicken stock*
*150ml (¼pt) velouté sauce*
*2 x 15ml tbsp (2tbsp) onion, very finely grated*
*2 x 15ml tbsp (2tbsp) double cream*

VELOUTÉ SAUCE
*25g (1oz) butter*
*25g (1oz) mushrooms, finely chopped*
*3 sprigs of parsley, finely chopped*
*25g (1oz) flour*
*300ml (½pt) strong chicken stock*
*2 green peppercorns*
*2 x 5ml tsp (2tsp) lemon juice*
*4 x 15ml tbsp (4tbsp) double cream*
*salt and freshly ground black pepper*

First prepare the velouté sauce. Melt butter in a saucepan. Add mushrooms and finely chopped parsley and fry gently for 5 minutes. Stir in flour and gradually blend in stock. Cook gently, stirring, until the sauce thickens. Add green peppercorns. Reduce heat and cover the pan. Simmer for 30 minutes. Strain and stir in lemon juice and cream. Season to taste. Leave to cool.

Now using a sharp knife, cut through the flesh on the breastbone of each chicken and carefully ease the flesh away from the carcass working downwards. Use the knife gently to scrape the flesh cleanly away. Remove each breast and take off the skin. Blot these four supremes dry with kitchen paper. Season well with salt and pepper. Using a small, heavy-bottomed frying pan, gently heat the butter until hot. Put the chicken pieces, outer side down, into the hot fat and cook for 4 minutes or until golden brown. Turn carefully, using a fish slice; do not pierce the flesh with a fork. Cook for a further 4 minutes.

Remove the chicken supremes to a warm serving dish and put into a moderate oven. Add the chicken stock to the pan juices, adjust the heat and reduce liquid by one half. Stir frequently, add the velouté sauce, finely grated onion and double cream. Heat through gently, pour over chicken supremes and serve immediately with boiled new potatoes and lightly steamed mangetout peas. Serve remaining sauce separately.

## ⊁ SYMBOL OF ⊁ EDWARDIAN ENGLAND

The lovely and delicate sweet pea was the flower symbol often used to represent Edwardian England.

# QUEEN MARY
*Wife of George V*
(1867–1953)

Princess May of Teck was born in 1867. She was the granddaughter of Adolphus, Duke of Cambridge, and daughter of Francis, Duke of Teck. Because her birth was in the month of May, the little princess was known affectionately as 'May-flower' or 'May-child', in place of her given names 'Victoria Mary'. These nicknames stuck and, to the British people, the Princess Victoria was always Princess May.

As children, Princess May and her brothers were encouraged to make little birthday gifts for Queen Victoria – a box painted with forget-me-nots, a china plate painted in gold or a fretwork basket. Needlework was also practised and the Queen received a hand-embroidered pocket-handkerchief case in May 1877 as a present from May, when she was

145

*Queen Mary*

just ten years old. This ability with the needle was put to good use, and from an early age Princess May was required to help with her mother's charity work. One of these charities was the Surrey Needlework Guild, which provided clothing for the poor.

Prince Eddy (Albert Victor), heir presumptive, became engaged to May in 1891, only to die six weeks later of an inflammation of the lungs. He was always considered delicate and was, in actual fact, quite backward and totally lacking in life. Physically he had an excessively long neck and was obliged to wear high starched collars, which earned

him the nickname 'Collars and Cuffs'. Recovering from this disappointment, May married Eddy's younger brother, George, Duke of York, in 1893. On the death of his father, Edward, George would become King George V.

At White Lodge in Richmond Park in spring 1894, Princess May, heavily pregnant, used to entertain for afternoon tea with a coverlet of white satin, embroidered with may blossoms, over her feet. The child she carried was to become King Edward VIII, for a short time, before the scandal of his abdication to marry Mrs Wallis Simpson.

At the time of the Durbar in India in 1911, Queen Mary enjoyed a Christmas in Rajputana, and in order to entertain her a small tiger hunt was arranged. A charming story is told of the Queen, sitting in a tree-hut knitting, pointing with her needle to an animal in the undergrowth and shouting 'Look, Lord Shaftesbury, a tiger'. It is pleasing to report that Lord Shaftesbury took so long in loading his gun that the tiger was able to turn away, disappearing quietly into the undergrowth.

At the outbreak of World War I, Mary's interest in knitting and needlework was put to good use. The old Needlework Guild was renamed Queen Mary's Needlework Guild, and groups of female volunteers were organised to knit socks and stomach-bands for the troops. So successful was the venture that it soon became apparent that these well-intentioned middle- and upper-class ladies were robbing their poorer sisters of their livelihood, as more and more women were dismissed from clothing factories. Orders dwindled until Mary Macarthur, champion of these working woman, begged influential friends 'to stop these women knitting!'

As she advanced in years, the Queen often rested before dinner, a lady-in-waiting reading aloud, whilst she herself took pleasure in a little embroidery. The outbreak of World War II resulted in the dowager Queen Mary moving to Badminton House, where she spent her days sorting out family papers and photographs. It was while she was here that she spent many happy and quiet hours working at her tent-stitch embroidery, and many chairs can be seen with seats and backs thus worked.

Mary died on the evening of 24 March 1953, at the age of eighty-five.

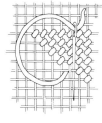

# ⊹Tent-stitch Embroidery⊹

Tent-stitch is sometimes referred to as 'petit point', particularly when it is very finely worked. The term 'petit point' once denoted all delicate white work as opposed to heavier stitchery, but over the years it came to mean any detailed counted-thread work.

# ⊹Beadwork⊹

Only beads which are sewn to a ground can be classed as embroidery. Beadwork dates back to the days of the early Egyptians, when beads were made of terracotta and turquoise. In medieval embroideries in Europe, semi-precious stones, coral and pearl were used in profusion. The Tudors and Stuarts made use of pearls and glass beads to decorate costume and stumpwork. Rich beading on open fabrics and net can also be achieved by using a tambour hook. This method of beading is still used by the fashion industry, as large areas can be covered in a relatively short space of time.

In Edwardian times elaborate beadwork was often used commercially with embroidery to decorate evening dresses and accessories, as can be seen by the wide use of seed and bugle beads on the daring flapper dresses of the 1920s.

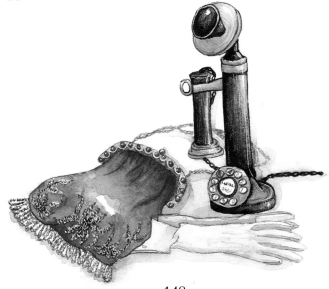

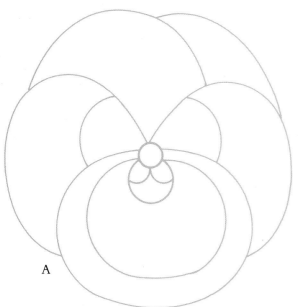

A

# Beaded Evening Purse

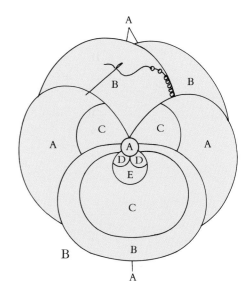

Small packets of seed beads:
*A black*
*B mauve*
*C transparent*
*D orange*
*E yellow*
*short beading needle*
*1 x 15cm (6in) diameter piece of linen*
*2 x 15cm (6in) diameter pieces of black velvet*
*2 x 15cm (6in) diameter pieces of
black lining material*
*1 large black bead or button*
*black and white thread*
*tracing paper*
*fabric marker pen*
*tambour frame*
*1m (1yd) black silk narrow cord*

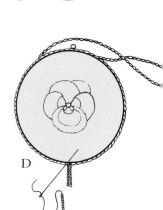

Using tracing paper, copy diagram A. Transfer the design to the linen, using the marker pen. Put the linen into a tambour frame, stretching fabric as taut as possible.

Following diagram B, attach beads in rows as shown below, building up the design. Start in the middle of the design, using white cotton, and bead the pansy petals, following the curve of each as you work. When the design is complete, trim off excess fabric, leaving approximately 7mm (¼in) all round. Turn under and tack, making sure no linen shows on right side of work.

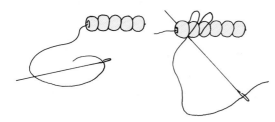

Machine the two circles of velvet together, right sides facing, leaving a gap of 9cm (3½in) for opening (diagram C). Stitch the linings in the same way. Turn velvet right side out, fit lining inside and hem a neat edge between velvet and lining at opening edge. Sew on cord, following seam around purse, continuing across opening and forming a small strap. Place beaded pansy in centre of purse and tack neatly into position. Finish by sewing on a bead or button in centre of opening and made a buttonhole-stitch loop on other edge to form a fastener.

Finally, make a fringe by threading 4 black, 2 transparent, 3 mauve, 1 black, 3 mauve, 2 transparent and 4 black beads onto a length of black cotton. Start at bottom middle edge, secure length of beads firmly with oversewing stitches (diagram D). Cut thread and repeat until fringe decorates lower third of purse.

## ⚜ SWEATED LABOUR ⚜

In Edwardian England, women were paid ¾d an hour for intricate sewing work, and blouses which were sold in fashionable Bond Street for 25s or more earned the workers as little as 6d per garment. The plight of these women was brought to the attention of the Queen by Mary Macarthur. The two women respected each other greatly and, after the reformer's death, Queen Mary became patroness of the Mary Macarthur Holiday Homes for Working Women.

## ⚜ THE QUEEN'S DOLL'S HOUSE ⚜

The Wembley Exhibition of 1924 contained a tribute to Queen Mary in the form of the Queen's Doll's House. This was the idea of Princess Aribert of Anhalt (Princess Marie-Louise). Queen Mary had a great weakness for miniature objets d'art and in view of this the family decided to ask Sir Edwin Lutyens to plan a doll's house fit for a Queen. Designed with a view to give future generations a glimpse of how a King and Queen lived in the twentieth century, it was also to be a show case for the artists and craftsmen of the day.

Many leading craftspeople and companies were delighted to be represented in this project. The garden was designed by Gertrude Jekyll, the dinner service was provided by Royal Doulton, and one patient woman spent an amazing 1,500 hours weaving the bed linen.

## ⚜ PRESSED FLOWERS ⚜

In February 1901, a sad token of remembrance was sent by Princess May to her Aunt Augusta. Flowers from the dead Victoria's bedroom had been pressed as mementoes for those close to her and in thanks Augusta wrote: 'Need I say, I wept over those flowers that had layed by Her side?'

Throughout her life Mary always loved cut flowers, her favourites being lilac, roses and lily-of-the-valley. Her drawing-room was always filled with their sweet fragrance, both in season and out, and this love of flowers can be seen reflected in her painting and embroidery.

# ⚹ A Twentieth-century ⚹ Wash Day

In 1911, Lever Bros, manufacturers of the famous Sunlight Soap, wrote to the Palace asking if Queen Mary were Empress of India. This information was, apparently, to be included in the advertising copy for one of their products. It was quite in order, at that time, for royalty to endorse commercial products.

## ⚹ The Common Touch ⚹

After a formal visit to a colliery in Wales, the Queen confounded officials by asking to be shown a typical miner's cottage. After much confusion, she was eventually taken into Mrs Thomas Jones's front parlour. The Queen was not satisfied, however, and insisted on seeing the kitchen where she apparently perched on an old kitchen chair, drinking a cup of tea. Poor Mrs Jones, overcome by the close proximity of royalty, insisted on giving her visitor an old mug to take home with her and the Queen graciously accepted.

*Kind, kind and gentle is she*
*Kind is my Mary*

Popular ballad

## ⚹ Marbled Paper ⚹

Marbled paper was immensely popular during Queen Mary's time. It was used in a variety of ways – to frame pictures, decorate boxes and, of course, as endpapers in good quality books. Paper marbling is an art and, as such, original examples are expensive to buy.

It is possible to produce your own designs at home with the minimum of equipment. It is great fun to do and the results can be quite spectacular. Try experimenting with a range of colours and techniques. Although paper marbling is relatively easy, it can be messy and so it is advisable to wear old clothes when working.

## To Make Marbled Paper

FOR SIZE
*28g (1oz) powdered gelatine size per*
*1 litre (2pts) water*
*½ litre (1pt) very hot water*
*½ litre (1pt) cold water*

*baking tray*
*selection of artist's oil colours*
*clean pots (one for each colour used)*
*½ litre (1pt) white spirit or paraffin*
*small paint brushes (one for each colour)*
*knitting needle*
*sheets of medium-weight good quality*
*white paper*
*old newspapers*

To prepare the size, sprinkle powdered gelatine into the tray. Pour on ½ litre (1pt) very hot (not boiling) water and stir well. When thoroughly dissolved add ½ litre (1pt) cold water and stir again. The size should fill the container to a depth of approximately 2.5cm (1in) and should still be fairly liquid. If it sets like jelly, it should be heated until liquid and a little more water added.

Select two or three oil colours and squeeze about 2.5cm (1in) from the tubes into separate pots. Dilute until runny with white spirit or paraffin. Using a paint brush keep the diluted colour well stirred. To test the strength of the colours and the size with which you are working, drop a spot of each colour on to the surface of the size. Each spot should float and spread to produce a circle of colour 1-3cm (½-1in) in diameter.

If a circle is too large, that particular colour is too runny; add more oil paint to the diluted colour in the pot. If the circle does not spread sufficiently, the mixture is too thick; add a little more paraffin or white spirit and try again.

When you are certain that the colours and size are well balanced, you are ready to begin marbling. The floating colours can now be arranged into a pleasing pattern by slowly drawing a knitting needle over the surface. The colours will not merge together, so intricate patterns can be produced.

When you are satisfied with the pattern, hold a sheet of paper for marbling carefully by its opposite corners and allow it to dip in the middle on to the surface of the size. Working outwards allow the paper to make contact, being careful that no air bubbles are trapped underneath. When the entire sheet has made contact, start at one edge and lift the paper gently. Hold it over the container for a few seconds to drain then place it, pattern upwards, on a sheet of old newspaper to dry.

# ⊁A Final Thought⊁

The great creative urge, which manifested itself so noticeably in Stuart and Victorian times, was to some extent halted by the outbreak of two World Wars. The resulting call to women to take their place in a working environment outside the home temporarily slowed their interest in most domestic crafts. However, as the twentieth century progresses, women are again finding themselves with a little time to spend on satisfying their need to improve and decorate the home, so that the sad prediction expressed in the quotation at the beginning of the last chapter of this book is proving, thankfully, to be based on a false premise. The skill and dedication of the women of Britain, of all classes of society, is an amazing tribute to their artistic ability from Norman times until the present day, and provides us with a wonderful heritage which we must strive to encourage and enrich as we pass our skills to our daughters.

*He who works with his hands is a labourer.*
*He who works with his hands and his head is a craftsman.*
*He who works with his hands and his head and his heart is an artist.*

St Francis of Assisi

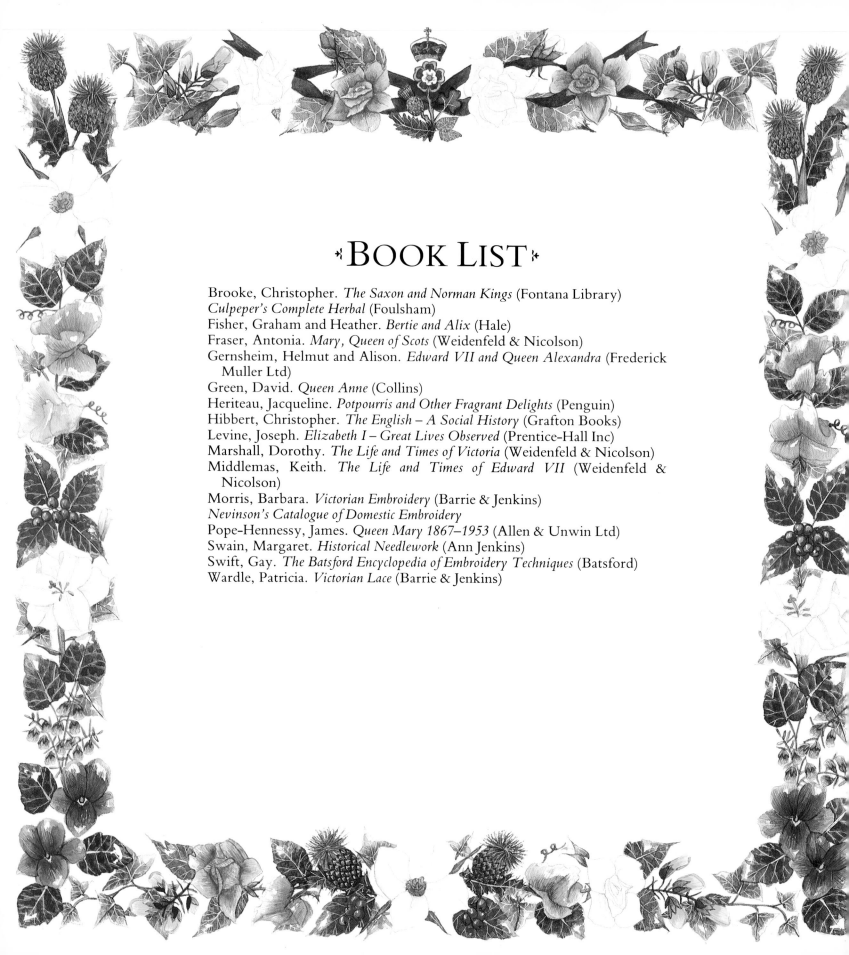

# ❖ BOOK LIST ❖

Brooke, Christopher. *The Saxon and Norman Kings* (Fontana Library)
*Culpeper's Complete Herbal* (Foulsham)
Fisher, Graham and Heather. *Bertie and Alix* (Hale)
Fraser, Antonia. *Mary, Queen of Scots* (Weidenfeld & Nicolson)
Gernsheim, Helmut and Alison. *Edward VII and Queen Alexandra* (Frederick Muller Ltd)
Green, David. *Queen Anne* (Collins)
Heriteau, Jacqueline. *Potpourris and Other Fragrant Delights* (Penguin)
Hibbert, Christopher. *The English – A Social History* (Grafton Books)
Levine, Joseph. *Elizabeth I – Great Lives Observed* (Prentice-Hall Inc)
Marshall, Dorothy. *The Life and Times of Victoria* (Weidenfeld & Nicolson)
Middlemas, Keith. *The Life and Times of Edward VII* (Weidenfeld & Nicolson)
Morris, Barbara. *Victorian Embroidery* (Barrie & Jenkins)
*Nevinson's Catalogue of Domestic Embroidery*
Pope-Hennessy, James. *Queen Mary 1867–1953* (Allen & Unwin Ltd)
Swain, Margaret. *Historical Needlework* (Ann Jenkins)
Swift, Gay. *The Batsford Encyclopedia of Embroidery Techniques* (Batsford)
Wardle, Patricia. *Victorian Lace* (Barrie & Jenkins)

# ✦Acknowledgements✦

The authors would like to thank the following: the staff of the Public Libraries of Birmingham, Lichfield and Burton-on-Trent for their patience and assistance in the face of what must have seemed, at the time, ridiculously obscure queries; David and Christine Springett for fan design and fan sticks (cover photo); Chris Davies for making the lavender batons; Graham and Carol Cartmell for the loan of the crazy patchwork quilt and postcards of the Royal Family; Simon Lings and Alan Greenman for the authors' photographs on the jacket; The Royal Archives for permission to reproduce items from Queen Victoria's Scrap Book; also Pamela Harper at Twilleys of Stamford in Lincolnshire and G. Baldwin & Co. Medical Herbalists, 173 Walworth Road, London, SE17 1RW, who have an excellent mail order business and will be happy to supply the ingredients required for many of the items featured in this book. Some of the projects in this book are available in kit form from Twilleys of Stamford Ltd, Roman Mill, Stamford, Lincs PE9 1BG (tel 0780 52661, fax 0780 65215, telex 32518 Twilly G). For further information send a stamped addressed envelope. In the USA these can be obtained from Scotts Woolen Mill, PO Box 1204, 528 Jefferson Avenue, Bristol, PA19007.

For their help in providing props and locations for the photography, the authors and publishers would like to thank Totnes Museum, Dawlish Museum, Cookworthy Museum, Kingsbridge, Bogan House Antiques, Fingles Hotel, John Prestige Antiques, Wendy Board, Forde House, Newton Abbot, Morris Tucker Antiques, and Paul and Barbara Heatley, Dartmoor Bookshop, Ashburton.

Thanks, too, to John Evans in Paris for his help in verifying and expanding on several facts, and to Judi Lang for trying out the recipes in her kitchen.★

And last, but not least, thanks to Pam Griffiths and Brenda Morrison at David & Charles for their kindness and encouragement in the production of this book.

★This footnote is provided for the sole use of Mr Ralph James of Lichfield – to do with as he will!

'Sound'

# ⊁INDEX⊁

*Whoever thinks a faultless piece to see,*
*Thinks what ne'er was, nor is, nor e'er shall be.*
*In every work regard the writer's end,*
*Since none can compass more than they intend;*
*And if the means be just, the conduct true,*
*Applause, in spite of trivial faults, is due (!).*

Alexander Pope
*Essay on Criticism*

*People who write books ought to be shut up!*

George V